At the Piano

Interviews with 21st-Century Pianists

Caroline Benser

THE SCARECROW PRESS, INC.
Lanham • Toronto • Plymouth, UK
2012

Published by Scarecrow Press, Inc.
A wholly owned subsidiary of The Rowman & Littlefield Publishing Group, Inc.
4501 Forbes Boulevard, Suite 200, Lanham, Maryland 20706
http://www.scarecrowpress.com

Estover Road, Plymouth PL6 7PY, United Kingdom

British Library Cataloguing in Publication Information Available

Library of Congress Cataloging-in-Publication Data

Benser, Caroline Cepin, 1944–
  At the piano : interviews with 21st-century pianists / Caroline Benser.
    p. cm.
  Includes bibliographical references and index.
  ISBN 978-0-8108-8172-3 (cloth : alk. paper) — ISBN 978-0-8108-8173-0 (ebook)
  1. Pianists—Interviews. I. Title.
ML397.B35 2012
786.2092'2—dc23
[B]   2011027519

Printed in the United States of America

Contents

~

Acknowledgments

My heartiest thanks go to the pianists themselves who most willingly and graciously shared considerable time and thoughts in the initial interview and in the dialogue of revision. And to the photographers for their outstanding photographs showing each pianist in the act of creating music at the piano: Xavier Antoinet; Greg Helgeson; Ben Ealovega; Grant Hiroshima; Jimmy Katz; Louise Narboni; and Raphael Stein.

Thanks go to Kathleen van Bergen and Sharon Carlson at The Schubert Club of St. Paul, Minnesota. The Schubert Club gave its kind permission to use Richard Sorensen's photograph of the stage at the Ordway Center for the Performing Arts in St. Paul. To Sandi Brown of the Minnesota Orchestra, which gave its kind permission for the use of Greg Helgeson's photograph of Sudbin performing with the orchestra.

Those who deserve many thanks for their help in putting this series of interviews together include: Charlotte Schroeder at Colbert Artists; Charles Cumella at Cramer Marder Artists; David Hooson at Harrison Parrott; Emma Sweetland and Lucy Jackson at Sulivan Sweetland; Angela Rance and Cate Dennes at IMG Artists, with Kathryn Endicott; Angela Duryea and Lisa Jaehnig at Shuman Associates; Mary Lynn Fixler at Barrett Vantage; Beth Kruse and Catherine Hampton at Hemsing Public Relations; Liz Chew and Laura Monks at EMI Classics; Lorna Aizlewood, VP, Legal and Business Affairs for EMI Records Limited (EMI Classics); Christina Jensen at Christina Jensen Public Relations; and Penelope Axtens at Sony International.

Many thanks to Bennett Graff, Christen Karniski, and Jessica McCleary of Scarecrow Press for the pleasure of working together.

Gratitude goes to colleagues and personal friends for their advice and suggestions: Eric Kraemer, James Wheat, and Deborah Buffton of La Crosse, Wisconsin, and Stephen Willier of Philadelphia. To Mary Goyette of the La Crosse Public Library for her help and countless courtesies. A big debt of thanks goes to Ann McCutchan of Denton, Texas, for her friendship and the earlier inspiration she passed along through her own absorbing series of interviews with American composers.[1] To Teresa Dybvig of Stony Brook, New York, for her long friendship, teaching, and expertise on healthy playing; she is more responsible for this book than she realizes. To longtime friend and pianist Dennis Eppich of Iowa City, Iowa, for his suggestions, helpful corrections, and gentle encouragement for many years. To Sue Hessel of La Crosse for her invaluable technological expertise and advice. And finally a special thanks to my husband, Jerry Benser, for his advice and enduring patience.

Note

1. Ann McCutchan, *The Muse That Sings: Composers Speak about the Creative Process* (New York: Oxford University Press, 1999).

~

Introduction

The eight pianists interviewed here, from my earliest interview with Leif Ove Andsnes in 2005 to my last with Yuja Wang in 2010, are representative of the finest pianists playing during the first decade of the 21st century. The choices are mine alone. My aim was to explore pianistic activity during this decade and, further, to explore aspects of life germane to this world. Who are the top pianists keeping good playing alive? Other questions came to mind: Are the masterpieces of several centuries of piano literature being well served by pianists who continue to discover fresh ideas about these masterpieces? Are older pieces of exceptional music being revived? Do contemporary composers find challenges in writing distinctively new, exciting music for pianists by working with them and, likewise, are pianists interested in commissioning and playing this new music? Are pianists in this decade drawn to being creative by composing, arranging, and improvising?

I have heard each of these exceptional artists in live performance, met each one, and listened closely to their recordings. Most of the interviews were conducted by telephone because it was convenient for both of us with regard to geography and their performing schedules. Having enjoyed their music-making beyond measure, I readily confess that I am an unabashed fan of each.

With the founding in 2005 of YouTube, the video-sharing website, pianists both historic and contemporary, are now seen and studied in video clips by thousands of viewers. Early on, these YouTube clips were quite short and made mostly by amateurs. Today lengthier and more professional clips are being uploaded and now join the earlier clips. During this decade, many pianists, including a number interviewed here, are writing blogs—online journals—on a variety of subjects on their websites. Some blog much more frequently than others. Stephen Hough continues to contribute regularly to his popular blog begun in 2008 for London's *Telegraph*.

Each pianist interviewed is known on the international musical scene, making appearances at the major recital and concert halls of the world, and participating in leading music festivals. They perform solo recitals, make concerto appearances with the world's major orchestras and conductors, and collaborate in chamber music performances with violinists, cellists, clarinetists, singers, and string quartets. As well, each maintains an active recording schedule. Several have joined noted musical institutions as teachers, which for some is in a limited capacity.

Each one was drawn well before the age of 10 to express his musicality through the awkward instrument that is the piano. Each has extreme technical facility. Each is an athlete of the small muscles of the hands and fingers. A high degree of personal discipline, along with a burning passion for their art, belong to each. Each knows he is doing the only thing in life that he must be doing. The only thing he can do. Much is accomplished in isolation, in focused listening. Sound is of paramount importance. Discovering how to create the sound heard in the inner ear is the work of a lifetime; thus, listening is important. Artistic originality requires serious study, thought, introspection, and scrutiny. Thus complete solitude and silence is necessary. Each is imbued with a high degree of musical imagination. He develops his own ideas about what he wishes to communicate about the music. Each plays the literature for which he has a strong affinity. He spends enormous time season after season stretching to learn music new to him, but it must be music he understands and loves. He constantly guards against falling into mere repetition. A fine performer does not hold back by being too conservative or cautious; he must be open to spontaneity. For that element of unpredictability, he must have loads of courage, self-confidence, and a willingness to rise continually to new challenges. He trusts his technical facility, his musical ideas, and his ability to communicate his personal musical intentions as well as those of the composer. And finally, each has the physical and emotional stamina required for the rigors of traveling and dealing with unexpected events that occur in the course of ever-changing travel schedules and closely scheduled performances.

These traits are balanced by shadows of self-doubt, a sense of vulnerability, thoughts of possible failure, and a large measure of humility. Each is aware that he is playing music that he can never get to the bottom of. The classic masterpieces he plays year after year require repeated new thought. Even today, there is no end to what can be discovered in studying and performing the music of Bach, Scarlatti, Haydn, Mozart, Beethoven, Schubert, Schumann, Chopin,

Brahms, and many others. The masterpieces of these composers are unfinished; they are open, and ever alive. Theirs is music that elicits new responses every time it is performed by the thoughtful performer. The English scholar Wilfrid Mellers was fond of saying that the classics are "News that stays news." [1]

Mozart's piano sonatas have long held pride of place on recital programs representing the height of the classical period, but many more pianists today are exploring the musical wit and imagination found in Joseph Haydn's amazing wealth of keyboard music, which includes over 50 sonatas. This discovery of Haydn did not happen overnight. András Schiff has long been dedicated to playing Haydn's music, and today Andsnes, Hamelin, and Sudbin gravitate with great liveliness to Haydn's music. Several pianists are musical sleuths, digging into 19th- and early 20th-century music that has lain dormant for decades and reviving it on stage and in recording. Stephen Hough, Marc-André Hamelin, and Steven Osborne play music that was once fashionable but fell out of favor. The music of Charles-Valentine Alkan, Leopold Godowsky, Ignacy Paderewski, Moritz Moskowski, Anton Rubinstein is occasionally heard now. Hamelin has recorded the music of the virtually unknown Gregoire Catoire, and Hough that of the equally obscure York Bowen. The music of Ives, Bartók, Janáček, Schoenberg, Berg, Webern, Messiaen, Ligeti, and Kurtág has appeared more and more frequently on their programs during this decade, and these pieces are becoming modern classics. This music is imaginatively juxtaposed with the well-known classics in order to give the listener a chance to hear the older classics in a new way and to present commonalities between the older and newer.

These pianists feel strongly about working with living composers, commissioning their music, learning it, and actively promoting it. Sometimes the listening public little understands the time and energy commitment required on a pianist's part to study and ultimately perform this new music. No pianist, however, would ever make a commitment to music about which he did not feel strongly positive. Without doubt the most active and creative performers on today's stages are those who become the strongest advocates of music being written today.

Finally, these pianists are themselves creative. Stephen Hough and Marc-André Hamelin are both highly competent composers and as well as arrangers of the music of others. Their scores are published so that others may enjoy them. They themselves frequently play their own music and have recorded much of it.

The creative art of improvisation suffered severe neglect through many decades of the 20th century. Many great pianists of the 19th and early 20th centuries improvised as a matter of course, but this skill went out of fashion as the obsession to follow the composer's every written wish had to be followed.

In a reversal, more pianists are improvising. Robert Levin, on the faculty at Harvard University, has long contributed his own cadenzas to his Mozart concerto performances, which was the standard practice in Mozart's own day. Noam Sivan, at Curtis, has founded workshops for improvisation for the students. Other notable improvising pianists include the Venezuelan Gabriela Montero, the Russian Denis Matsuev, and the Turkish Fazil Say. Notable among Americans are the highly inventive Stephen Prutsman, and jazz pianists Marcus Roberts and Keith Jarrett (b. 1945). Osborne has credited Jarrett with being an influence on his improvising.

Considerable attention throughout the interviews is given to the earliest memories of each pianist's coming to the piano, of being encouraged and strongly supported by family, and the all-important subject of their teachers. Not a single one of these exceptional pianists sprang out of nowhere. Talent aside, they are the product of a nurturing home environment plus excellent teaching and guidance over many years by generous teachers who made a tremendous impact.

Simone Dinnerstein spoke at length in her interview about her study with the late notable Italian teacher Maria Curcio (1918–2009). For many of the pianists interviewed, especially Jonathan Biss, an equally exceptional teacher is the American Leon Fleisher (b. 1928). Both Curcio and Fleisher were students of the great Beethoven pianist and teacher Artur Schnabel (1882–1951). Through these two Schnabel students, his spirit continues to live into our century through yet another generation. Not to be overlooked is the fact that both Curcio and Fleisher shared experiences of physical and emotional suffering that impeded their performing careers but ultimately led to their intense devotion to teaching.

Fleisher deserves attention for two reasons. First, he has had an enormous impact as a teacher at both the Curtis Institute in Philadelphia since 1986, and since 1959 at the Peabody Conservatory in Baltimore where he has long made his home. His influence has extended to many highly gifted pianists playing today, including Jonathan Biss, who speaks most highly and appreciatively of his mentor. Other pianists playing today who studied with Fleisher include André Watts, Lorin Hollander, Yefim Bronfman, Louis Lortie, and Stephen Prutsman. Fleisher also deserves attention because his particular case as an injured pianist has attracted much media attention over four decades. While his case is just one among many pianists who fall victim to debilitating finger, hand, and body injuries, it is important because it has been highly public and has helped in large measure toward leading to a vastly proliferating body of literature and analysis in the world of both music medicine and teachers of body movement as it relates to playing the piano.

Fleisher grew up in San Francisco and as a child studied with the great Beethoven pianist Artur Schnabel. It was with Beethoven's music that Fleisher himself became most closely associated when he blossomed as a young performing pianist. No doubt, he has passed down his Beethoven genes, most notably to Biss. In 1964 at the age of 36, Fleisher was preparing for a tour of the Soviet Union with the Cleveland Orchestra when he was struck by a physical debility that eventually came to alter his life's work as a performer. He noticed that two fingers of his right hand began to curl under uncontrollably. There was no pain, but within a few months his right hand was useless as a pianist for he had developed a debilitating neurological disorder. For 30 years, Fleisher sought help from entities as diverse as the medical community, Rolfing, acupuncture, hypnosis, and Zen Buddhism.

In order to remain grounded in the musical world, Fleisher turned to conducting and held several posts during the era when he played exclusively as a left-handed pianist. The Ravel Left-Hand Concerto became a staple of his repertoire. He also began his own search for new and exciting literature, commissioning a wide variety of composers to write concertos and solo works for the left hand, expanding this repertoire greatly. William Bolcom, Lukas Foss, Leon Kirchner, Curtis Curtis-Smith, George Perle, and Gunther Schuller[2] have written for Fleisher. Bolcom's *Gaea* from 1996 is distinctive in that it is for two pianos, two left hands, and orchestra, and is written so that it may be performed in a variety of combinations. Bolcom composed the work for both Fleisher and Gary Graffman, also at Curtis. Graffman as well has spent a large part of his performing career as a left-handed pianist.[3] Schuller's Concerto for Piano Three Hands from 1990 is for two pianos with chamber orchestra, written for Fleisher and Lorin Hollander.

In 1991 Fleisher's condition was formally diagnosed as focal dystonia, which is characterized by involuntary, uncontrolled movements of the muscles of a finger or several fingers. Focal dystonia is task specific, and not only a concern of the muscles of the fingers, but also of the hands. In the 1990s, when Botox was gaining attention as an agent in cosmetic medicine for alleviating wrinkles, Fleisher was encouraged to try it. Injections were administered into the muscles of his right forearm. Although Fleisher struggled for years with the idea of injecting poison into his body, he did find that his hand responded positively. He was absolutely ecstatic when he was able to use his right hand once more at the piano. By the end of 2010, Fleisher had already played programs with both two-hand and left-hand literature for over a decade. It should be clear, however, that Botox is not a cure for focal dystonia. Its effect wears off and it must be administered on a regular basis for its alleviating power to remain effective. As well, there are some individuals who cannot tolerate it. [4]

Today there is a wide range of opinion in two different worlds regarding the root causes and most effective treatment of focal dystonia. The world of playing pianists and the sciences that study body movement are on one side of the issue, and on the other side there is the medical world with its researchers and practitioners. Each side has vastly differing opinions within it. The questions surrounding whether it can be completely or partially cured by any means are subjects for frequent discussion at piano seminars, workshops, and programs. The medical world is also trying to find whether it can be cured by any means. Because focal dystonia also plagues office workers who spend long hours at a computer keyboard, it is now recognized as an occupational health hazard. This is the same affliction called writer's cramp that strikes accountants and writers who use pencils and pens for long hours at a stretch. Whether poor technique, poor posture, emotional stresses and strains, A-type personalities who strive for perfection, genetic factors, or simply fate contribute singly or jointly toward dystonia's development, it continues to be analyzed and studied by both the piano and medical worlds at an ever greater pace today. Among musicians, there is only speculation on the number of pianists who suffer from focal dystonia. In the medical community, however, Eckart Altenmüller, who is an active pianist as well as a medical researcher and practitioner at the Hanover Institute for Musical Physiology and Musicians' Medicine, suggested in a 2003 breakthrough article that perhaps 1 in 200 musicians may well suffer from focal dystonia. Injured pianists hope that further research and collaboration will allow development of effective treatment and even prevention.[5]

In addition to the subjects of teachers and the special health problems pianists encounter, there are other topics relevant to the decade under consideration. Many of these subjects are touched upon throughout the interviews but deserve more attention here.

China is just such a subject, as today it plays a huge role on the world's musical stage. Yuja Wang, interviewed here, represents China's cultural role among this group of pianists. The phenomenal rise of China and its whole-hearted acceptance of Western musical culture since the end of the repressive Cultural Revolution in 1976 is nothing short of eye-opening. The last two decades of the 20th century and into this century have presented the world today with a glut of young, overachieving pianists who enter competitions showing off that each winner can play faster and with more technical facility this year than the winner in the previous year's competitions. In the middle of the decade it was estimated that as many as 50 million Chinese were studying music and among those were 36 million studying the piano. Many Chinese parents began to move to Beijing and Shanghai to live in crowded conditions so that their children could study in the best musical schools. As well, the Chinese government sponsored many of their most talented young musicians in programs for study abroad. And later, Chinese parents began to move to Europe and the United States with their young children, one to a family, so that the young musicians could study in the foremost music schools of the West. So many of these students were in the United States that it led Robert Sirota, president of the Manhattan School of Music, to remark in 2007: "I honestly think that in some real sense the future of classical music depends on developments in China in the next 20 years." He went so far as to predict that perhaps in 20 to 40 years Shanghai and Beijing may well be considered the centers of the world of music.[6]

The Chinese pianist Lang Lang's (b. 1982) American concert debut in 1998 unleashed a torrential stream, often called "The Lang Lang effect," of young Chinese pianists seeking study in the United States and indeed in all of the West. A short time earlier, in 1997, Lang Lang had become a student of Gary Graffman at the Curtis Institute, from which he graduated. As the decade progressed he became a global product. In China he is revered as a national hero, as evidenced by his appearance at the opening of the Olympic Summer Games in Beijing in August of 2008. If he chooses, his playing can be tenderly poetic. Throughout the decade, however, his innate musicianship too often became overshadowed by his formidable technique, which he pressed into service in whiz-bang, faster-than-fast, louder-than-loud, exaggerated performances full of facial mugging, grandstanding, and look-at-me antics that have been highly criticized in the press.[7] Whatever may be said for his pianism, musicianship, and his overly dramatic performance demeanor, his role as a strong advocate for bringing thousands of young people into concert halls worldwide to hear good music is invaluable. The Lang Lang International Music Foundation, to which Lang Lang himself devotes time, works tirelessly to bring young children to music.

Lang Lang is by no means the first Chinese pianist to figure prominently in the West. Fou Ts'Ong (b. 1934), who was born in Shanghai, lives and teaches today in London. He studied in Warsaw in the 1950s, becoming China's first internationally celebrated pianist, known as "China's Chopin," after winning the Chopin Competition. He makes an appearance in Sudbin's interview.

Not to be overlooked is Yin Chengzong (b. 1941), who risked his life in 1967 to save pianos from destruction during the Chinese Cultural Revolution. In Beijing's Tiananmen Square, he played his piano, a Western instrument, clearly seen as a protest symbol of the Mao regime's ban on the instrument. His message was that pianos would not be obliterated from China by Mao's call for their destruction. Later, in 1970, he composed the piano part of the now-famous *Yellow River Concerto* and further made his career playing and teaching in the United States. In May of 2010 he made a concert tour of China in commemoration of his stand in 1967. Certainly this stand is one factor that contributed toward the amazing proliferation of today's estimated 30 million Chinese children studying piano.[8]

Yet another subject is that of the instrument of the piano itself and the question of favoring one instrument over another. Pianists have long favored one instrument over another. The American Steinway, established in New York in 1853, and the Hamburg Steinway, established in Germany in 1880, have long held pride of place as the leading choices of the professional pianist. To a lesser degree and for varying reasons, the instruments built by Bösendorfer, Blüthner, Bechstein, Grotrian, Baldwin, Kawai, and Yamaha have long been widely known and favored. At the same time, there are today a number of pianists who find themselves drawn to the particular qualities found in the newer Italian Fazioli instrument. And the even newer Australian Stuart piano is slowly gaining attention. Both of these instruments are exceedingly expensive as they are handmade, built from specialty woods and other products, and in limited supply.

In 1978 Paolo Fazioli (b. 1944), himself a pianist as well as an engineer, gathered about him several teams of experts knowledgeable in the physics of sound, top-quality woods, and metals. By early 1981, the business of Fazioli Pianoforti was established. During the 1980s the piano was introduced throughout Germany, Austria, and Italy by pianists including Aldo Ciccolini, Alfred Brendel, and Murray Perahia. Interest in the instrument spread globally, and Fazioli continued to open new showrooms in more and more cities. Production, which has always been quite small compared with other makers, has grown to the level of about 100 instruments a year, with about 1600 having been built by the middle of the first decade. There are four models, the largest of which is the F308, which runs 10 feet 2 inches long. It has a fourth pedal which brings the hammers close to the strings; this decreases the volume while allowing the normal tone of the sound to remain. Many remark on its responsive action. Fazioli's growth eventually necessitated new production facilities, and by 2000 a new factory was begun. In 2004 its new office areas and the Fazioli Concert Hall were completed. The business celebrated its 25th anniversary in the fall of 2006 with festivities at its facilities in Sacile, near Venice.

Fazioli's strongest advocate is the Canadian pianist Angela Hewitt (b. 1958) who bought her first Fazioli in 2003. She developed a close working relationship with Paolo Fazioli, who subsequently became one of the sponsors of her 18-month Bach World Tour in which she had played both books of Bach's *Well-Tempered Clavier* in 58 cities in 21 countries by the end of October of 2008. Most of these recitals were on a Fazioli. Hewitt is drawn to the Fazioli's range of color and bright clarity which is suitable for her vision of Baroque music. Her first recording on a Fazioli in 2004, however, was devoted to Chopin's nocturnes and impromptus.

In 1990 Wayne Stuart established his new piano instrument business, Stuart & Sons, headquartered in Newcastle in New South Wales, Australia. To date, fewer than 100 instruments have been produced, but they are found throughout Australia, North America, Europe, and Asia. Stuart pianos were exhibited at the Shanghai World Expo in 2010. There are several different models of the Stuart, one of which has 102 keys. Up to this point, no other piano had been built with over 100 keys. Stuart's expansion of the keyboard is found in both the bass and treble registers and is currently presenting a fascinating challenge to composers to write for such an expanded keyboard.[9]

The standard keyboard has 88 keys. Today Bösendorfer builds two models. The earliest is the Imperial Model 290 which has 97 keys, making a full eight octaves. This instrument was first built at the suggestion of Ferruccio Busoni (1866–1924) when he requested the extra bass register keys for his Bach transcriptions. By 1900 Bösendorfer had entered the Imperial model into production. Other 20th-century composers have also written for the Imperial 290, chief among whom is Bartók who uses this extended keyboard in his 1926 Sonata, and later in both his Second and Third Piano Concertos. Bösendorfer also builds the Model 225 with an extended range in the bass that adds 92 keys to the standard 88.

Angela Hewitt's remarkable playing of Bach's music has been a major hallmark of this decade. Earlier she spent a number of years recording all of Bach's music, including the concertos with the Australian Chamber Orchestra. Wigmore Hall and the Fondation Hoffmann underwrote a commissioning project that enabled her to request several contemporary composers to write short pieces based on Bach's music for her. Hewitt's idea followed up that of the English pianist Harriet Cohen (1895–1967) who commissioned a number of her contemporaries to write arrangements based on Bach's music for her. *Harriet Cohen's Bach Book* appeared in 1932. *Angela Hewitt's Bach Book*, published in 2010, contains arrangements and new compositions.[10]

The astounding French pianist Pierre-Laurent Aimard (b. 1957) has increasingly become a widely admired presence at the piano during the first decade. Aimard has long felt a strong responsibility toward the living composer, and indeed to all composers. For him the composer is always first, while the performer is second. At age 12 he began his serious study of music with Olivier Messiaen, and at age 19 he joined Pierre Boulez's Ensemble InterContemporain when it was founded in 1977. With this experimental group in Paris he early came into contact with the music of the Hungarian composer György Ligeti (1923–2006). Later he developed a close working relationship with Ligeti who composed his now-famous set of études from 1985 to 2001. Most were written for Aimard who has become known for playing them. Today Ligeti's 18 études are considered masterpieces from the late 20th century. Aimard later developed personal relationships with György Kurtág (b. 1926), George Benjamin (b. 1960), Harrison Birtwistle (b. 1934), and Elliott Carter (b. 1908), and is closely associated with playing their music, as well as that of his compatriots Messiaen and Boulez. Bach, Beethoven, Ravel, Debussy, Mozart, Liszt, Berg, among many others, have each held Aimard's attention, as he is now known for his adventurous programs juxtaposing widely diverse older and newer music. His programs delineate for audiences the commonalities of music that is sometimes centuries apart.

Other equally exciting pianists making fine music and who bear watching and listening to include Piotr Anderszewski, Lise de la Salle, Jeremy Denk, Ingrid Fliter, Paul Lewis, Lars Vogt, and Shai Wosner. Among the earlier generation of those who continue to play imaginatively and have consistently explored new music are Emmanuel Ax, Imogen Cooper, Richard Goode, Murray Perahia, Garrick Ohlsson, Maurizio Pollini, András Schiff, Jean-Yves Thibaudet, Mitsuko Uchida, and Krystian Zimerman.

In a world devoted largely to entertainment, technical gimmicks, and celebrity, we can thank these artists for upholding the highest musical standards. They continue to welcome us into the sanctuary of the concert hall. Their performances slow us down, connecting us with our inner selves so that we can find stillness in the midst of our noisy, frantic lives. Perhaps in emerging from this refuge after a performance, we will have found transcendence and communion with the sublime through their art.

Notes

1. Mellers paraphrases Ezra Pound's much-quoted line: "Literature is news that stays news," found in his 1934 collection of essays, *ABC of Reading*. Mellers makes an appearance in Hough's interview.

2. Bolcom (b. 1938); Foss (1922–2009); Kirchner (b. 1919); Curtis-Smith (b. 1941); Perle (1915–2009); Schuller (b. 1925).

3. Gary Graffman (b. 1928) studied at Curtis, and joined the faculty in 1980, later going on to leadership positions. In 1979 he injured the fourth and fifth fingers of his right hand and was diagnosed with focal dystonia. He, like Fleisher, has commissioned a number of compositions for the left hand alone, and has led an active career as a left-handed pianist, in addition to his major role as a teacher.

4. Leon Fleisher and Anne Midgette, *My Nine Lives: A Memoir of Many Careers in Music* (New York: Doubleday, 2010). Here one can see a 1938 photograph made in Lake Como showing a group of Schnabel's students, including the 10-year-old Fleisher seated beside Maria Curcio.

5. Considerably more emphasis is being devoted today to teaching beginning students, and indeed all students, how to use the body correctly in order to avoid habitual misuse of the body. One of the more notable teaching methods began to be codified by Dorothy Taubman (b. ca. 1918) in the 1960s. She gave one of the first public presentations on her thought in 1969. She has since passed her teaching on to her principal exponent, Edna Golandsky, who in 2003 founded the Golandsky Institute at Princeton University. Taubman advocated for efficient, coordinated movement at the piano, teaching the student to use the body efficiently in order to avoid injury caused by repetitive movement. Golandsky has since trained dozens of pianists with the Taubman method.

Among the third-generation of Taubman-trained pianists are several who have had considerable success as dedicated teachers helping students to improve their playing by simply teaching them healthy keyboard habits. One of these teachers, Teresa Dybvig, who is also a performing pianist, suffered extensive injuries but was able to recover through personal trial and error to improve the quality of her movements at the keyboard. For 20 years now, as a teacher, she has worked with injured students and has been able to help many overcome a wide variety of serious injuries and return completely to successful playing. Several of these have recovered after long suffering with focal dystonia. In retraining with focal dystonia, the teacher works with a trusting student who travels a road with perseverance and an open mind about his body. He learns how to give up his old habits and to develop a keen awareness of his body's movements. The condition is not cured; he must be ever alert to his body use in order to maintain healthy playing. Dybvig continues to teach all her students—injured or not—Taubman's basic tenets of alignment, balance, and coordinated movement and has added yoga, Feldenkrais, Alexander Technique, and Aston-Patterning to her teaching. To these, she also gives attention to practice and performance mind-set exercises at her Well-Balanced Pianist workshops.

6. Daniel Wakin, "Chinese Musicians Hitting a High Note in the West," *The New York Times*, 3 Apr. 2007.

7. David Remnick, "The Olympian," *The New Yorker*, 4 Aug. 2008. This is a lengthy profile, chiefly featuring Lang Lang's appearance at the Beijing Summer Olympics.

8. Nancy Pellegrini, "The Man Who Saved the Piano for His Country," *International Piano*, no. 1 (May/June 2010), 14–15.

9. For those who would like to hear the sound of a Stuart & Sons instrument, Simon Tedeschi plays a program recorded over several days in January 2000 at the City Recital Hall, Angel Place, in Sydney, Australia, released on a Sony Classical CD. He plays the fourth instrument produced by Stuart.

10. In 2010 Hyperion released a 15-CD set of Hewitt's complete recorded Bach solo music. Boosey & Hawkes published *Angela Hewitt's Bach Book*, containing transcriptions and three original compositions by Brett Dean, Robin Holloway, Elena Kats-Chernin, Dominic Muldowney, Kurt Schwertsik, and Yehudi Wyner.

Leif Ove Andsnes. © Ben Ealovega licensed to EMI Classics

CHAPTER ONE

~

Leif Ove Andsnes

Leif Ove Andsnes was born on the island of Karmøy near Haugesund south of Bergen on Norway's rugged west coast on the 7th of April in 1970. Both of his parents were teaching musicians. Although his youth may not have appeared particularly special with regard to his musical abilities, he did gain national recognition in Norway's Youth Piano Championship competitions quite early, the first time in 1979. He also received support from several Norwegian scholarships and grants.

But it was in 1998 that Andsnes, without winning a single major international piano competition, found himself in the international spotlight after being awarded the Gilmore Award. This noncompetitive award is presented every four years by the Gilmore Award committee of Kalamazoo, Michigan, to honor a well-developed pianist who shows distinct potential for an international career. Those who are chosen do not know that they have been watched for several years. The award carries a monetary prize of $300,000. Only $50,000 is given in cash and the remainder is set aside for projects. Andsnes bought a new instrument with his cash.

While still in his teens, he had already distinguished himself by winning the Hindemith Prize in 1987 during his years of study with the Czech pianist Jiři Hlinka at the Conservatory of Music in Bergen. At just age 20, in 1990, he won the prestigious Grieg Prize. In the same year, his recording of the Grieg concerto with the Bergen Philharmonic spread his artistry beyond Norway.

Andsnes has thus remarkably made his way representing his small home-land country to which he continues to feel a distinct connection. After playing at the Risor Chamber Music Festival for two years in the early 1990s, he was asked to join the violist Lars Anders Tomter as his co-artistic director in 1993. Held in the small fishing village of Risor on the southeast coast of Norway, the festival has presented Norwegian performers such as the cellist Truls Mork and the pianist Håvard Gimse along with Emanuel Ax, Gidon Kremer, Maxim Vengerov, Steven Isserlis, Matthias Goerne, and Joshua Bell. For a number of years, the festival concentrated on presenting many largely unknown Norwegian composers, but soon the programming turned to featuring contemporary composers, with each year's festival being built on a theme. The weeklong Risor Festival has become one of Europe's principal festivals in the last few years, as it takes place at the height of the summer season when the sun shines well into the night, and concerts are heard around the clock.

Andsnes was chosen as the youngest and first Scandinavian to hold Car-negie Hall's prestigious Perspective Series of seven concerts for the 2004–2005 season. His goal was to present eclectic programs of music about which he feels most passionate. Working with a roster of his favorite musical partners, including the English tenor Ian Bostridge, the German violinist Christian Tetzlaff, and a wide variety of his favorite Norwegian performers, including the Norwegian Chamber Orchestra, Andsnes fashioned programs devoted both to well-known and virtually unknown composers. Listeners found themselves, for example, hearing works as varied as Bach's F Minor Concerto and Mozart concertos with the Norwegian Chamber Orchestra; the music of Schumann, Dvořák, and Janáček; the Hungarian György Kur-tág; and the Danish composer Matthias Ronnefeld.[1]

Since 2002 Andsnes has been designated the first guest conductor with the Norwegian Chamber Orchestra, a group with which he both plays and conducts from the keyboard. In 2006 he led the group on a U.S. tour play-ing two different programs devoted to Mozart and Haydn concertos, as well as several Beethoven works. They have toured together throughout Europe each season since 2008. Both soloist and orchestra are known for their highly acclaimed Haydn and Mozart recordings.

Ample proof of Andsnes's voice in bringing life to the contemporary composer is found on his EMI Classics recording from 2009 of selections from György Kurtág's *Játékok (Games)*, Dalbavie's concerto, and Bent Sørensen's[2] *Shadows of Silence* and two *Lullabies*. On the heels of this well-received recording, his *Pictures Reframed*, juxtaposing both older and contemporary music, later generated widespread discussion.

At the keyboard one finds a quiet, serious pianist, utterly devoted to music. Neither artifice nor wizardry inspire his keyboard demeanor. Andsnes has commented that for him the ritual of going on stage, experiencing the silence while approaching the piano, is almost a holy act. He believes strongly in his connection with his audience. He has played in major festivals such as the Edinburgh, Aspen, Ravinia, Saratoga, and Tanglewood. His solo recital appearances have taken him to Berlin, Copenhagen, London's Wigmore Hall, Amsterdam, and many cities throughout the United States. Andsnes has collaborated with the best orchestras and conductors around the globe. He is loved by Japanese audiences, and has toured throughout that country at least 10 times since he was 23. He played with the Tokyo Philharmonic under Mikhail Pletnev in his 2005–2006 tour. To give an idea of his cult status in Japan, in February of 2007 five Japanese newspapers reviewed his recitals to great acclaim, with one paper granting him a five-page spread. His concert attire is courtesy of the Japanese fashion designer Issey Miyake. Andsnes was the subject of a segment for England's *South Bank Show*, a television arts program, which documented him on film in the autumn of 2001. Needless to say, he is beloved in his home country. In 2005 Astrid Kvalbein's biography *Leif Ove Andsnes: I og med musikken* was published.[3]

During 2007 Andsnes devoted himself to learning the Brahms Second Concerto for the first time, and played in October under the fiery young Venezuelan conductor Gustavo Dudamel[4] with the Orchestre Philharmonic de Radio France in Paris. Earlier, in May, in two separate concerts, he played Lutoslawski's concerto[5] and Marc-André Dalbavie's[6] concerto, which was written for and dedicated to him. Andsnes gave the world premiere of Dalbavie's music at the London Proms in 2005. Both of these works were recorded in a live performance with Franz Welser-Möst and the Bavarian Radio Symphony.

Since our conversation, Andsnes accepted a part-time professorship in the fall of 2007 at the Norwegian Academy of Music in Oslo, teaching two young pianists—one from China and one from Albania. He is presently also Visiting Professor at the Royal Danish Academy of Music in Copenhagen. He continues to seek advice from the Belgian teacher Jacques de Tiège.

Andsnes has paid special attention to recording the music of his fellow countrymen, in particular that of Edvard Grieg, from his earliest release of the popular A Minor Concerto on Virgin Classics in 1990. He returned to the work in 2004 with the Berlin Philharmonic, and garnered a Gramophone Award for the best concerto recording of 2004. His 2002 release of a selection of Grieg's *Lyric Pieces*, which he performed on Grieg's own Steinway in Troldhaugen became a best seller, and won a Grammy Award for the Best

Instrumental Recording of the year. In 1997 Andsnes recorded a number of smaller pieces by Norwegian composers of the 20th century including Geirr Tveitt, Fartein Valen, and Harald Saeverud[7] along with some of Grieg's folk songs, on his recording *The Long, Long Winter Night*. In 2006 Andsnes took part in an invaluable conversation about Grieg with Rob Cowan of *Gramophone*[8] magazine. They covered the composer's nationalism, the influences on his music, and discussed the several versions and revisions of the concerto. They discuss not only the piano music but also much of his other music, and one clearly sees the pianist's connection to his compatriot. Andsnes briefly touches on Grieg's largely neglected Ballade in G Minor, which is essentially a set of variations on a Norwegian folk tune—a work he later learned. Andsnes admitted the work is awkwardly written in places and required some skill to find solutions to some of its clumsy pianistic writing, but because it is not currently in the repertoire of pianists beyond Norway, he felt it was his time to learn the dark work. He recorded it to coincide with the commemoration of the 100th anniversary of the composer's death in 2007. Andsnes took part in a documentary, released on DVD, that follows Grieg's footsteps during the time of the composer's crisis in later life. Some of the final scenes show a piano being hoisted up by a helicopter over the breathtaking scenery of Norway's Hardanger Fjord, with Andsnes later playing the instrument, perched dramatically on the edge of a cliff. Andsnes laughingly admitted later that the instrument was a terrible one, used just for this dramatic scene. After filming, he wanted to push it over the edge, but was not allowed.[9]

November 2009 saw the premiere at Alice Tully Hall of *Pictures Reframed*, a collaboration between Andsnes and the South African videographer Robin Rhode. At the conclusion of Rhode's film this same piano met its demise by drowning.[10] The project featured Andsnes performing Mussorgsky's *Pictures at an Exhibition* in front of five large panels of video art illustrating Rhode's pictures. The entire "performance" also involved a new commission, *What Becomes*, from the Austrian composer Thomas Larcher[11] as well as Schumann's *Kinderszenen*. Afterward, the multimedia production embarked on a world tour, followed by the release of the production on both CD and DVD.[12]

At the top of Andsnes's recorded legacy are his four Schubert recordings of sonatas and lieder with the English tenor Ian Bostridge, with whom he began a collaboration in 2001. Andsnes has long had a genuine fondness for Schubert's music and had planned for some time to record the sonatas. After he worked with Bostridge at Risor, the two decided on a joint effort devoted to Schubert. Three of their recordings couple one of Schubert's major late piano sonatas with selections from the lieder, while their 2004 release is devoted to *Winterreise*.

Among honors awarded Andsnes is his designation as Commander of the Royal Norwegian Order of St. Olav, received in 2002. In 2007 he received the Peer Gynt Prize, whose honoree is chosen by members of Norway's parliament.

In June of 2010, Andsnes's daughter Sigrid was born to him and his partner, Ragnhild Lothe, who plays the French horn with the Bergen Philharmonic Orchestra. Andsnes also relinquished his directorship of the Risor Festival that year in order to spend more time with his family.

Andsnes was modest and easily approachable in conversation as I spoke by phone with him during his time in Kansas City, Missouri, on the morning of the 24th of January in 2005.

Interview

Did you always know that you wanted to be a pianist when you were younger?
No. But not because I wasn't working on music, or that I didn't want to play, but I wasn't surrounded by professional musicians, though my parents are music teachers. And I'm from a small community. I didn't know what it was to be a professional musician, or a professional pianist. I guess I had an idea I would have to work with music in my life. It was always a very serious thing for me when I sat down at the piano, but I didn't have any clear idea about the future or what it would bring. Only when I was 13 or 14 did I think there wasn't much of a way back. I had to follow this route now. But I really found myself when I was 17, and made my recital debut and first recording. I thought suddenly—I am a pianist now. I hadn't realized it before then.

Were you with Jiři Hlinka[13] by that time?
Yes, I met him when I was 15, and he was my main teacher. I studied with him for 10 years and still have the occasional contact with him. Something clicked between us. A teacher like him is not necessarily good for everybody, but there was something that I needed so much from his personality. I think I already had a very natural, basic finger technique. When I came to him my touch was natural, but I was a rather shy person, rather an introvert. He was rather the opposite. I needed that kick. Also the whole attitude about music: that this is really about life and death, isn't it? It is very important. Music is something so burning inside. I had it inside but it didn't naturally come out. So I remember the first couple of years when I started working with him

he always said, "When you play something through, you always start tenta-tively, then when we start working, it gets so much better. It's like I have to warm you up!" And, you know, he was right! That helped. He also stressed the whole physical aspect of playing. He was very influenced by the Eastern European Russian school in thinking that what you're feeling inside should correspond with the physical movements of your body when you play, which is important.

Did you play much Czech music with him?
I did actually, especially in the beginning. Janáček is a composer who I've continued to play because I absolutely love him. I remember when my teacher sat down at one of the first lessons I had with him, he played one of the shorter piano pieces. I said, "What is this? It's so beautiful." I had never heard of Janáček. So I started playing all that piano music with him and made one of my first recordings with Janáček's piano music. But in addition to that, I've played some Smetana. Some of his Czech dances, polkas, and the grand concert study *On the Seashore*. I've played parts of the *Poetic Tone Pictures* of Dvořák, which I absolutely adore. It's wonderful music! Hlinka would always go on about Martinů, but I wasn't so keen on him. And although I know Joseph Suk's music, I haven't played it.

Did you suggest Smetana's one-movement piano sonata[14] that you played at the Verbier Festival Piano Extravaganza in the summer of 2003?
No, I'm sorry. I would love to give you that! The organizer of the festival came up with that.

Was Hlinka behind your love of Haydn's music?
Yes. He was going on about Haydn's sonatas. He is not so much a Mozart man, and I think that was reflected in those early years, as well. He em-phasized Haydn and Beethoven more than Mozart and Schubert. So, yes, I started playing Haydn sonatas with him. I think he's wonderful, and his sonatas are so valuable.

Hlinka himself released a recording of some of Haydn's music about 10 years ago, didn't he?
That's right. He had a physical problem when he came to Norway, but then he improved about 10 or 12 years ago and began making a couple of record-ings. But he's not playing so much again now.

Have you played Mozart's sonatas very much?
No, I haven't. I feel that I will get to his sonatas later in life. At the moment I'm so in love with his concertos, that I'm gradually expanding my repertoire with those. That is fine for me at this point. Thinking about other composers, I have devoted a lot of time in the last few years to Schubert, and I'm still doing that. I also want to study Schubert's C Minor Sonata, which I've not done yet. After that I really want to get on with Beethoven because he is a much more urgent case for me. I do feel that that is what I really want to do. I have done a bit of Beethoven. A while ago I played the Second, Third, and Fifth Concertos and I've played five or six sonatas. I've now had a few years away from Beethoven.

You started out playing Grieg's A Minor Concerto, and you've recorded it twice. How do you keep a work like this concerto ever fresh?
I've always found that I find myself bored when I have to practice it again. I just know that it is a piece where there are difficult things. You have to work on it. You can't just let it go. But on stage—live—I have never been bored with that piece. I've always found that it is so fresh. It has a beautiful mixture of childlike beauty, a sort of innocence. It is the work of a man who wanted to show the world what he wanted to do, but it is also very temperamental with very big gestures as well. It is a wonderful mixture. It became the one large-scale work that became his big success. One does understand why. Because it contains wonderful harmonies, and all the transitions are so well done.

His *Lyric Pieces* are such gems. Thanks to you, we are able to hear them played so wonderfully on his own Steinway on your recording devoted to Grieg. We realize all too clearly that they are not merely teaching pieces.
They are very special in their way. Almost without exception they are built on the same ABA form. But within that simplicity, there are such special harmonies that Grieg himself wouldn't know where they came from. It's a special sound world as well. It's probably a mixture of things. Certainly not just Germanic, because there is something there that comes from French music. For example, a piece like his "Bell-ringing"[15] is like an early Impressionistic piece before Debussy. In fact, a couple of years ago I played a program where I put a few Grieg pieces together with Debussy's music. I played the Grieg *attacca*, going straight into one of Debussy's studies. That was very effective because they belonged to the same sound world.

Are there composers whose work you would like yet to explore?
I absolutely adore Debussy's piano music, and that is something I would love to do so much. So his music is very much on my to-do list. I want to do some Bach, but I haven't gotten around to doing much yet because he demands time to study. I'm playing contemporary music, which is something I really want to do.

Tell me about Bent Sørensen's *Shadows of Silence,* which the Carnegie Hall Foundation commissioned expressly for you and which you premiered.
I think Sørensen is a very special composer as I knew many of his pieces. I chose him to compose the commission because I admired him, not because he was a friend at that time. He's become a good friend through this process. *Shadows of Silence*[16] is very unusual because when I first saw the score I thought, "Oh, this is not very pianistically written. This is hard work." And it was hard work to study it. But it turns out that it is a great piece for the piano because it uses the piano's low bass register a lot. There are very shimmering qualities created by lots of repeated pianissimo notes, which makes it difficult. And then it has this bell-ringing sound from the bass. It's very evocative of the cool landscape of Scandinavia.

Also at the moment, the French composer Marc-André Dalbavie is writing a piano concerto for me. It's a co-commission among the Proms in London, the Cleveland Orchestra, and the Chicago Symphony. Dalbavie was the resident composer for a couple of years with the Cleveland Orchestra about five or six years ago, and he's now the composer with the Orchestre de Paris. He's a very interesting composer in his mid-40s. I will play the premiere in August this year with the Proms. I haven't yet seen any of the music. I have to say it's very exciting to play something which nobody has heard because there is a freedom in it. There is no burden of tradition or interpretation. When you play it, you can basically do whatever, if the composer agrees. In a way, one should be as open to any classical piece of music. Right? I mean the problem is we have too many recordings in our ears. The tradition of interpretation can be difficult sometimes. Therefore I think it is a worthwhile lesson to study contemporary music. Also for me, I would feel funny if I didn't play any modern music. I'm a child of my time, and I want to see what's going on today with music. It's so lazy for pianists not to do it because there is so much great repertoire for the piano.

Among the older generation of pianists, whose playing do you admire?
I'm happy to say I went through different phases. My teacher was influenced by the Russian piano school. For him, Richter and Gilels were the great

heroes and they became for me also. Especially Richter. When I was about 20, I couldn't listen to any other pianist because I was completely obsessed by Richter. He was such a great personality, had the most phenomenal talent, and played so much of the repertoire. When everything worked, it was incredible. But I've come to like and to love very different types of pianists. I think Michelangeli[17] in some repertory is absolutely incredible, especially Debussy. One special favorite of mine is Géza Anda[18] who I think is such an underrated pianist and a great musician. A lot of young people don't know him. There was such a natural way of making music in what he does. He was spontaneous, so alive, totally without makeup, and so honest. Without being shy, he takes risks. His playing is a wonderful combination of intellect and intuition. And, of course, I adore Lipatti, the best of Schnabel, and Horowitz at his best. He orchestrated at the piano.

I want to talk about spontaneity in performance, live on the stage. You've been on the international scene now for about two decades, so I'd like to know how you consistently create the feeling that you are spontaneously creating the music you know so well.
It is always something that one hopes will happen. Sometimes you just feel that you are doing what you have planned to do, but, yes, in a good concert you feel that you are creating the piece in the moment. That's the kind of feeling that we strive for on stage. For me, it doesn't mean that I have to have an attitude of being free and in the moment, but what I mean is actually preparing everything meticulously. Only if you have a framework and if you have a perfection of the finger work and the movement, then you can feel really free.

Where do you find the best listeners in the world?
Obviously there is a tradition in central Europe for this music that you cannot underestimate. You just feel that if you are playing for an audience, say, in Vienna, that they know a lot of the music of Beethoven, or Schubert. That music is not the most spectacular, sound-wise or in virtuosity. But it demands a certain understanding in some pieces, and you feel with that audience that they know this music. That is a wonderful feeling because then you feel that they can be attentive to all the details with you. Details such as shadings and color in your playing.

Do you play in Asia and in Australia frequently?
I do the occasional tours there. I've been three times in Australia. And I've done maybe eight or nine tours to Japan, sometimes including other Asian

countries. I'm now going in February on a tour with the Norwegian Chamber Orchestra to Seoul, Shanghai, Kuala Lumpur, and Hong Kong. It is interesting how that market seems to have expanded in the last 5 or 10 years. It used to be very centered around Japan and Asia. But Japan has had difficult times in the last 10 years with decreasing audiences. Probably due to a lot of financial difficulties, but also because the audience for classical music has more problems there than it used to. But then there are other countries that have really come up, so it's very interesting and exciting. I'm curious about what will happen in China in the next decade when it really starts exploding. I'm sure there will be a huge audience there in a couple of decades. You feel the energy coming from there. I especially remember Seoul where 80 or 90 percent of the audience was teenagers. Especially teenage girls. I was signing autographs and CDs in the lobby after the performance and there was screaming [*laughs*]. I felt just like Elvis! That is a very different environment from the normal one, and that is fun! It is really wonderful that there are so many young people coming to concerts.

What about South America?
I did do one tour with the BBC Symphony and was to go back last fall for recitals, but unfortunately I got sick. It's an amazing experience to play in the Teatro Colòn in Buenos Aires. It is one of the largest in the world, holding 3,000 people and they do fill it for piano recitals with a nice mixture of both younger and older people.

Have you had experiences with poor behavior on the part of an audience?
One wants one's audience to be quiet but sometimes that is a problem. There was one audience in Manchester, England, where I was starting a recital with some of the *Lyric Pieces* by Grieg, and there was a lot of coughing. One person who clearly had a bad problem continued to cough for the first 10 minutes. I couldn't believe this person wasn't leaving, as it was getting so bad. After the fifth of these pieces, I stood up and said, "I'm really sorry, but I have a great problem concentrating so I will go out and have a little break." So the person with the cold can try to sort it out. I got a huge applause, of course! If you treat it like that you get applause, and afterward you have the best audience. They're sure to be quiet. One has to be careful, because one shouldn't be rude to an audience. They've paid to listen to you. Actually one of the biggest problems in a concert hall is a hearing aid that is making a very high-pitched noise. You have to be careful what you say because normally that person doesn't hear it. And cell phones are an

especially big problem in Europe. I haven't had such a problem with that in America and don't know why.

What about humorous experiences during a performance?
I was playing the Grieg concerto in Latvia on a tour with the Norwegian Chamber Orchestra when after a few seconds the pedals fell off [*laughs*]. It wasn't a very good instrument in the first place. Someone came and repaired it. So that was rather funny. There's not much you can do about that!

You've mentioned the Teatro Colòn in Buenos Aires. Do you have any favorite halls with regard to the sheer quality of the sound?
Yes, I do have. In the case of a couple of the legendary halls, it also goes with the audience, like the Musikverein in Vienna. The Concertgebouw in Amsterdam is particularly good for piano recitals. Carnegie Hall's sound itself may not be on the same level, but it's amazing that you have such a big hall which sounds so good. I just played a recital there five days ago, and it is an interesting experience that you have this sort of intimacy in a hall which seats about 2800 people. It is wonderful. There are less famous halls—but absolutely beautiful—like the Musikhalle in Hamburg, which is perfect for piano recitals. It's exciting that there are new halls being built now, such as the one made out of light wood in Zaragosa, Spain. I don't know why it works so well, but it's incredible. And there are, of course, small halls like London's Wigmore Hall which I like very much. Maybe even more is the Mozart Hall in the Konzerthaus in Vienna. That may be my favorite chamber hall. In Japan there is the Suntory Hall in Toyko. Orchestra Hall in Detroit, which I absolutely love in America, sounds so well.

How do you stay in shape mentally and physically to counteract the stresses of modern traveling?
Like many, I'm trying to stay reasonably well in shape, but I don't have any regimen. I have started in the last year to do some yoga. This is in reaction to the fact that 10 or 12 years ago I developed some physical problems in the shoulder, and at one point I felt pain. I've been through Alexander Technique and some very different holistic therapy, acupuncture, as well as Chinese medicine. I believe in lots of things. Yesterday I went down and did a half hour on the treadmill to get the heart going. I just came from Europe; I was in Venice where I walked for two days. It was pure joy. I'm trying, but I'm a little bit lazy! Mentally it is very important for me to have a feeling that I have a base, a home. I don't have a family myself but I have three younger

sisters and parents, and they are very important to me. They are sort of spread out and don't live near me.

Are you still living in Bergen?
I live in Bergen, but that is not where I grew up. I began living there when I was 16 because I was studying there with Hlinka, and I have lived there since. But also for the last seven years I have had an apartment in Copenhagen. It might sound very impractical, but the little time I have when I'm not on the road I am dividing myself between these two places. It is very important for me as I have very close friends in both places. With a very few, I keep in regular contact. It is important in this life to have a feeling of home. Then also, I have a house in the mountains where I love to go skiing in the winter and hiking in the summer. I have an electronic piano there so that I can even work there. Part of the reason I am still living in Scandinavia is because I am very drawn to its nature, and it's very important to me.

And of course you spend a busy time during the summer in Risor where you are the artistic director of your chamber music festival, and participate in numerous chamber music groups. Let's talk about the activities there.
Yes, we have very specific themes. Last year we did lots and lots of Schumann. For the next two years we will do lots of Mozart. And we combine that with other composers who are less featured, like Richard Strauss and a few contemporary composers. We invite the artists and ask them to suggest some composers. We're very open to suggestions!

Do you have plans to make live recordings sometime?
A lot has been recorded, but I have mixed feelings about that because I do feel the musicians should be feeling very free, not having the pressure of live recording hanging over them. We have been thinking about doing one project with parts of the Norwegian music we've played over the years now because we have played lots of Norwegian composers over the years.

Composers most of us don't know.
Yes. That might be interesting for a double CD.

Do you have ambitions to conduct away from the piano some day?
I don't have any ambitions, but I sometimes have a lot of desire. But then I think: There is so much piano repertoire to work on. I won't rule out the possibility, but for the moment, no.

Is there anyone you would like to collaborate with but have not had the chance at this point?

I am very lucky doing about two chamber music projects a year, meaning two tours. And I have Risor. I normally do one or two events in the summer which include chamber music. I am not looking for other partners because I find that it's sad that the friends I am doing chamber music with I see so rarely. In addition to Bostridge and Tetzlaff, I've done some things with the baritone Matthias Goerne. The cellist Henrich Schiff is another good friend of mine. I'm planning to do the Brahms quintet with the Artemis String Quartet for the first time this year.

Is there a particular orchestra and conductor you'd like to team with but haven't had a chance at this point?

Yes, I have not played with the Vienna Philharmonic and I will make my debut with them and Mr. Harnoncourt next year. I am looking forward very much to meeting the orchestra and the conductor. One conductor who I have sometimes adored listening to is Abbado, and I've never played with him. That would be wonderful.

What about teaching?

The only teaching I do at the moment is the occasional master class; I'm doing one today. I might have a teaching position some day, but now that feels like a rather foreign thing to me simply because of time.

You've so much piano repertoire yet to explore.

Yes [*laughs*]. You can't start teaching before you've done that!

I thank you so very much for sharing your thoughts this morning.

You're welcome.

Select Discography

Sergei Rachmaninov. Concerto # 3 in D Minor, op. 30; Concerto # 4 in G Minor, op. 40. London Symphony Orchestra. Antonio Pappano, conductor. EMI 4051162B. 2010.

Pictures Reframed. Modest Mussorgsky. *Pictures at an Exhibition. Memories of Childhood.* Schumann. *Kinderszenen.* Studio recording. EMI 983602B. 2009. *Shadows of Silence.* Bent Sørensen. Two Lullabies. *Shadows of Silence.* Witold Lutoslawski. Piano Concerto. Marc-André Dalbavie. Piano Concerto. Live performances with the Bavarian Symphonic Orchestra. Franz Welser-Möst, conductor. György Kurtág. Selections from *Játékok*. EMI Classics 2-64182 2. 2009.

Franz Schubert. Piano Sonata in C Minor, D. 958. Allegretto, D. 346. Allegretto, D. 900. Andantino, D. 348. Lieder, including three *Gesänge des Harfners*. Ian Bostridge, tenor. EMI Classics 3843221-2. 2007.

Robert Schumann and Johannes Brahms. Schumann's E-flat Major Quintet, op. 44, and Brahms's F Minor Quintet, op. 34. With the Artemis String Quartet. Virgin Classics 0094639514328. 2007.

Horizons: A Personal Collection of Piano Encores. Twenty short works. EMI Classics 41682. 2006.

Sergei Rachmaninov. Piano Concertos # 1 and # 2. Berlin Philharmonic. Antonio Pappano, conductor. EMI Classics 7243 4 74813 2 1. 2005.

Edvard Grieg and Robert Schumann. Piano Concertos, both in A Minor. Berlin Philharmonic. Mariss Jansons, conductor. Grieg is a studio recording; Schumann recorded live in Berlin in 2002. EMI Classics 557562-2. 2004. Gramophone Award for Best Concerto in 2004.

W. A. Mozart. Concerto in E-flat, K. 271. Concerto in B-flat, K. 456. Andsnes, piano and conductor. Norwegian Chamber Orchestra. EMI Classics 24355 78032. 2004.

Edvard Grieg. *Lyric Pieces*. Selections from op. 12; op. 38; op. 47; op. 54; op. 57; op. 62; op. 65; op. 68; op. 71. Recorded in 2001 at Troldhaugen in Bergen on Grieg's 1892 Steinway. EMI Classics 72435 57296 2 0. 2002. Gramophone Award in 2002.

Franz Schubert. Piano Sonata in A Major, D. 959. Lieder selections. Ian Bostridge, tenor. EMI Classics 2435-57266-2. 2002.

Franz J. Haydn. Concertos. # 3 in F Major; # 4 in G Major; # 11 in D Major. Andsnes, piano and conductor. Norwegian Chamber Orchestra. EMI Classics 7243 5 5690 2 1. 2000. Gramophone Award in 2000.

DVD—Filmography

Pictures Reframed. Modest Mussorgsky. *Pictures at an Exhibition. Memories of Childhood.* Schumann. *Kinderszenen.* Videography by Robin Rhode. Hardcover book also included in limited edition with DVD. EMI 670052B. 2009.

Ballad for Edvard Grieg. Documentary on Grieg's life and music commemorating the 100th anniversary of the composer's death. EMI Classics. 2008.

Leif Ove Andsnes Plays Mozart. Concertos # 9 in E-flat Major, K. 271, "Jeunehomme"; # 18 in B-flat Major, K. 456; # 20 in D Minor, K. 466. J. S. Bach. Concerto in F Major. Andsnes, piano and conductor. Norwegian Chamber Orchestra. Interview with Andsnes discussing Mozart. Filmed live in Oslo's Posthallen in 2004. EMI Classics 0946 3 10436 9 7. 2005.

The Verbier Festival and Academy 10th Anniversary Piano Extravaganza. Filmed live in Verbier, Switzerland, 22 July 2003. RCA Red Seal. Andsnes was one of 10 pianists participating. 2004.

Notes

1. Matthias Ronnefeld (1959–1986).

2. Bent Sørensen (b. 1958).

3. Published by Det Norske Samlaget (trans. *Leif Ove Andsnes: In and with the Music*).

4. Gustavo Dudamel (b. 1981) became the director of the Los Angeles Philharmonic in fall 2009.

5. Written for the Polish pianist Krystian Zimerman in 1987 and later recorded by him.

6. Marc-André Dalbavie (b. 1961). French composer who studied with Boulez and is part of today's "spectral" movement in France.

7. Geirr Tveitt (1908–1981); Fartein Valen (1887–1952); Harald Saeverud (1897–1992).

8. Rob Cowan and Leif Ove Andsnes, "The Real Grieg," *Gramophone Collector's Edition* CD, Aug. 2006, 55 minutes.

9. David Weininger, "For One Piano Master, a Balancing Act," *The Boston Globe*, 4 Jan. 2008.

10. The old instrument was later dried out and installed in the lobby of a radio station in Bergen.

11. Thomas Larcher (b. 1963).

12. See www.picturesreframed.com.

13. Jiři Hlinka (b. 1944) in Prague. He began his professorship at the Music Conservatory in Bergen in 1972. He continues to teach. In honor of his many contributions to teaching, the Czech Republic honored him in 2007 with its distinguished Jan Masaryk Award.

14. Smetana's Piano Sonata in E Minor, for two pianos, eight hands. This performance is part of the Verbier Festival DVD.

15. *Lyric Pieces*, op. 54, # 6.

16. *Shadows of Silence*, a 16-minute work dedicated to Andsnes, occupied Sørensen for five years.

17. Arturo Benedetti Michelangeli (1920–1995). Italian pianist.

18. Géza Anda (1921–1976). Hungarian pianist known especially for his Mozart concertos for which he composed many cadenzas.

Jonathan Biss. Photo by Jimmy Katz

CHAPTER TWO

~

Jonathan Biss

Jonathan Biss was born on 18 September 1980 to two professional-musician parents, both on the faculty at Indiana University in Bloomington, Indiana, where the young pianist came of age in a musical milieu. Biss has stated on several occasions, however, that he was in no way a child prodigy. Later, as music and his life as a pianist took on a more serious role for him, his parents cautioned him about life as a performing musician. While they did not promote his life in music, they did not discourage him either. His early life in out-of-the-musical-spotlight Bloomington could not have been more ideal, he now readily admits, as it allowed him to work and explore unpressured, at his own pace. Today he realizes that he was allowed to choose his own path; it was not thrust on him. As a result, he feels acutely how lucky he is today to be doing what he loves.

By the time of his birth, his mother, Miriam Fried (b. 1946), had already established herself as a highly regarded violinist, most notably by becoming the first woman to win the Queen Elizabeth International Competition in 1971. She came to the United States from Israel under the mentorship of Isaac Stern, studied at the Juilliard School with Ivan Galamian, and then went to study with Joseph Gingold at Indiana University. She later received high praise for her 1985 New York recitals of Bach's solo *Partitas and Sonatas*, and in 1986 she joined the faculty at Indiana University. She has for many years played chamber music, solo recitals, and performed concertos with a number of major orchestras worldwide, and is a highly regarded recording artist. She joined the Mendelssohn String Quartet as its first violinist in 1999, and in the fall of 2006 she joined the faculty at the New England Conservatory of Music in Boston. Fried and her son have long been chamber music partners, and are frequently heard in all 10 Beethoven violin sonatas. He has joined her in working with the Mendelssohn String Quartet.

Paul Biss, the pianist's father, is a violist and violinist well established in musical circles, having worked with his wife and many others. He is retired from Indiana University but continues to teach. It was Paul Biss's mother, the noted cellist Raya Garbousova, whose name and place in American music history continues to be noted without fail in the pianist Biss's biographical notes. She was one of the world's most eminent cellists when Samuel Barber wrote his cello concerto expressly for her in 1945. She premiered the work with the Boston Symphony under Serge Koussevitsy in 1946, and 20 years later recorded it for Decca. Garbousova was born in Tbilisi, Georgia, in 1909, and came to this country in 1939. After marrying the cardiologist Kurt Biss in 1948 and settling in DeKalb, Illinois, she taught at Northern Illinois University from 1979 to 1991. She died in 1997 when Biss was 16. He speaks of her with a tinge of regret in this interview.

Bloomington, Indiana, may have been off the high-pressure musical path in some respects, but his parents' connection to well-known musicians in the world beyond Bloomington made his home environment a singularly musical one. As a youth he did not realize this, but he certainly does now. At that time it was a normal home for him. His mother's mentor, the violinist Isaac Stern, was often a guest in their home and later he heard Biss, at age 14, play in Israel. Stern became a close personal friend of the young Biss for six short years, until Stern's death in 2001. Stern was responsible for finding professional management for Biss with ICM Management at the youthful age of 16. This meant that Biss was a full-fledged professional musician for a year before his arrival at the Curtis Institute where he studied with Leon Fleisher. Like dozens who have benefited from Fleisher's wide musical knowledge and keyboard wisdom, Biss speaks highly of his mentor at every opportunity.[1]

In speaking with Biss, one is forcibly struck by his utter devotion to performing the music of those composers for whom he feels a strong passion. He is adamant about playing only music for which he feels the greatest connection. He has gone so far as to resist making a career by performing the big audience-pleasing works, famously turning down a performance with a major orchestra because he did not feel committed to playing Rachmaninoff's *Rhapsody on a Theme of Paganini*. He has performed Rachmaninoff's Second Concerto, a work he admits is beautiful but would not find it lacking in his life if he never performed it again.

There is a large enough body of piano literature that holds a lifetime of challenges for Biss. This is the music that is far greater than he will ever be able to perform to his final satisfaction. It is the music that he never wants to feel completely satisfied with after a performance. And the music that he will never tire of exploring, keeping vital for himself and his listeners.

At the top of his list is the music of Schumann, Beethoven, and Mozart. His love of Schumann's music extends to his having performed the seldom-heard Introduction and Allegro appassionato, op. 92, and the Introduction and Concert-Allegro, op. 114, both for piano with orchestra under Daniel Barenboim with the Staatskapelle Berlin in Chicago in January of 2004. Biss's love of Schumann's later music extends as well to the composer's Second Violin Sonata in D Minor, op. 121, which he plays frequently with his mother. Schubert and Brahms are in his pantheon as well. He frequently programs Janáček's *In the Mists* and his *Sonata, Oct. 1905*; Schoenberg's *Sechs kleine Klavierstücke*, op. 19; Berg's *Sonata*; and Webern's *Variations for Piano*, op. 27. Bartók's Third Piano Concerto likewise holds his interest as Bartók is for him one of the major composers of the twentieth century.

Biss is committed to playing music by contemporary composers, including the American elder statesman Leon Kirchner whose work Biss discovered when they worked together at the Marlboro Music Festival. He has programmed Kirchner's 2003 Second Sonata a number of times, played his 1989 *Interlude I*, which was written for Peter Serkin, and finally Kirchner's *Interlude II*, of which Biss is the dedicatee. The work was commissioned by the BBC's New Generation Artist program expressly for Biss. The work began life as a piece for left hand alone for Leon Fleisher, who many years earlier had also championed Kirchner's music. Among other contemporary composers whose music he plays are Toru Takemitsu, Wolfgang Rhim, John Corigliano, Richard Danielpour, Lewis Spratlan, and David Ludwig.[2]

Biss is not a showman at the piano. He has nothing to prove. He is all about the music. Unpretentious and secure in his well-thought-out musical ideas, his communicative skills afford him the ability to bring the most inward, introverted music to the listener in an unhomogenized performance. For him, performances should not feel routine, but special, otherwise he does not want to play. His strength lies in revealing the musical architecture of a whole piece in performance. He pays special attention to his programming. A program of several Beethoven sonatas will be presented in an order that takes the listener on a journey. His tall body is lanky, and at the keyboard his breathing can be quite noticeable, as it is also in the recording studio.

Biss's maturity includes thinking about his future as far as 50 years hence. He takes seriously the idea that how he plays today is not as important as how he will play when he is in his 70s. For him, being a musician is not a static stage at which one has arrived, but a lifelong process with which one grapples daily. A musician's life is constantly evolving. Part of Biss's own evolution involves joining the piano-teaching faculty at Curtis in the fall of 2011.

We spoke at length about the Borletti-Buitoni Trust he was granted several years ago. Biss has also been the recipient of other notable awards and honors, including the 2002 Gilmore Young Artist Award, an Avery Fisher Career Grant, and the Leonard Bernstein Award at the Schleswig Holstein Music Festival in 2005. He was the first American to participate in the BBC's New Generation Artist program, a two-year program that Biss held from 2002 to 2004, and which coproduced his EMI Debut recording in 2004. Having received so many notable honors for his active performing life, it is surprising that Biss did not give his first solo recital at Carnegie Hall until the 21st of January, 2011.[3]

I spoke with Biss by phone on 1 July 2007 at his New York City apartment as he was nearing the end of his summer break from performing.

Interview

Thanks so much for agreeing to be a part of my project. Several years ago it became very clear that there are many excellent pianists playing today keeping alive the best literature from Bach's music down to the end of the twentieth century. Now that we've entered the 21st century, I considered taking a serious look at who is playing, and exploring the details of what is happening around the globe.
Certainly, I'm so glad you feel that way.

I want to compliment you on your recent recording of Schumann's music. Your *Kreisleriana* performance is especially wonderful with regard to your phrasing and pacing that are so inevitable.
Thank you. That's the nicest thing I could possibly be told.

When we think about what you have right there, in that recorded performance—which you obviously prepared very well—we still want to know how much of that performance is spontaneous on your part in the studio. Or do you have in mind presenting this performance as a recorded artifact?
Right. I don't think that would even be possible. Even if you wanted to, you couldn't go into a recording with the idea that "I want to play exactly like this." More importantly, I don't think one should want to. The only way I find recording to be a gratifying process is to think of it as nothing more than

a snapshot of what your thoughts about that piece of music were that day. And obviously you can't plan for what your thoughts about the piece are going to be that day. It has to do with who you are when you wake up that morning. When you choose to make a recording, it is not just a question of choosing pieces that you can play well and that you feel prepared with, but pieces that you feel that you have an actual relationship with, and finding pieces that your thoughts and ideas about are constantly in evolution. Those are the pieces you're going to feel a degree of inspiration of feeling in playing when you're in this somewhat sterile environment of the recording studio and where the audience is not immediately visible. The biggest challenge of recording is creating the feeling that something is being communicated, which is probably the most important element in a successful performance at any time. Above all, my goal for recording is to create the feeling of a performance in which something speaks.

When playing for an audience, most of it is obviously very spontaneous.
Absolutely. It has to be. Again, it has to do with the pieces you choose to play. You have to play pieces that you feel closely enough connected to, so that you are confident enough to be spontaneous and that the decisions you make spontaneously will be true to the music. These decisions will reflect the effect of the music. At least personally, I don't find I'm free enough to take chances and try some things if I don't feel a profound connection to the music. If you're being the vehicle of a piece that you have loved, then you feel that you can have free rein with your personality to take you in whatever direction you'd like that particular evening. A recording really should be the same thing.

Pieces do have different ways that one can look at them. Maybe one year you would want to bring out one thing, and in another year, you may chose to bring out something else.
Absolutely. I think almost by definition great music is music that has numerous aspects and layers so that the more you delve into it, the more you see and the more you're able to do with it, and the more you realize there is so much more left to be done. With this music that you know well, understand its essence, its basic architecture, and where the essential points are, you know that there are an infinite number of possibilities you can do while holding true to the music. I don't ever think of it as being limiting, though you do have to respect the intention of the composer. Great music can accommodate many different intentions, as long as at the core you have an understanding of what the piece is about.

This is why when we hear the same Beethoven sonata in the hands of five different pianists, the performances can be totally different.
Yes. Music is a three-way interaction between a composer, an interpreter, and an audience. All three pieces of the triangle are essential ones. The way that the three interact with one another creates the whole. It's amazing how the notes on the page of a Beethoven sonata have never changed, and they're not going to change, but when pianists take those pieces up, those pieces do somehow evolve. Which is kind of a miraculous thought.

I want to go back to your earliest studies at the piano. You began at age six and were influenced early on by the playing of your older brother, Daniel.
That was probably the reason I started playing the piano. I think I was four when he started playing the piano at age six. I don't remember this, but apparently that is the story.

How far did he go in his study?
Pretty far. I think he was 13 when he gave it up, and he was quite advanced. He's come back to it, and I would say he's an excellent amateur pianist. I don't think there was ever any question in his mind about wanting to do it professionally. It was something that he enjoyed and I would certainly describe him as a music lover. I don't think he ever dreamed of doing it professionally himself.

What did he go on to do?
He's a mathematician.[4]

Quite a few medical doctors start out as very keen pianists, and drop it to go into the medical profession. Later, they turn around and spend five years returning to the piano. We know Drew Mays[5] who won the amateur Van Cliburn Competition just a few weeks ago.
And a doctor!

Yes, an eye doctor. We knew him when he was a piano student at the University of Alabama in Tuscaloosa. He gave up the piano for 15 years but returned to practicing as an example for his four children.
Very, very interesting. My brother has many, many friends who are not only mathematical but in the broader scientific community. Often when I play concerts he brings friends with him. It's amazing to see how interested they are, and how lively is their interest in music. There is some kind of connection between the two.

Yes. Did you ever play duets with your brother?
Oh, very, very little. I think my parents very wisely thought that we were best separated. I think they really didn't want either of us to ever see music as competitive.

Are there other siblings?
No, just the two of us.

You soon went to Karen Taylor,[6] who was in Bloomington at Indiana University.
Yes, she was my very first teacher. She was the person in Bloomington who taught young children. She was extremely good with younger children especially. She had many students who were at the high school level as well as beginners. It's such a specific ability to be able to reach a small child on a musical level and to teach basic skills to a child whose attention span is not incredibly highly developed. She was really fantastic at it. She managed to teach those skills, all the while really making it something that a child could love. I remember having a lot of enthusiasm for music, not just for playing the piano. I owe a lot of credit to her.

Those beginning teachers are so important.
Absolutely. Now I've come to a point where I sometimes give master classes at places where I am giving concerts and frequently find young pianists who are talented, but I can tell that they're not being taught. I think there's a lot of variation, speaking of technique, in terms of what can work on the piano—depending on the size and shape of your arms, and the rest of your body, and also depending on what sort of a sound you're looking at. But there are also basic principles which I think are universal—to do with relaxation, breathing, use of the arm to support the fingers, etc. And sometimes I see students who have so many problems in these areas, it's completely interfering with their ability to express themselves. And it's such a pity, because it's so much easier to learn those things initially, than to have to unlearn something else and start from scratch after you've already been studying for years. Good teaching really is invaluable. I always wonder when I see someone who is already 13 or 14 if their problems are reparable anymore.

It could be, but it would take a tremendous amount of willpower on the part of the person to want to change.
And initiative.

This is a topic for an hour's discussion! Going back to your studies, you next went to Evelyne Brancart[7] during your teen years. How old were you when you went to her?
I think I was 11. I was with her until I went to Curtis when I was 17. So it was six years that I spent with her.

Do you remember what you first studied with her?
I remember the pieces that I played at the end of my first year at her little recital. I played the Haydn E Minor Sonata, the Chopin *Bolero*, which is a piece I don't think I've even heard since!

Chopin's *Bolero*?
Yes! I'm surprised I even remember that. I do remember looking at it once in a volume of miscellaneous pieces and thinking, "I played this." And I played Liszt's *Au bord d'une source* from the *Première Années de Pèlerinage* and Mozart's K. 467, the C Major Concerto. It's hard to imagine that I played those pieces, but it was after a fashion, anyway.

I suppose you have tapes of those.
My parents must.

Maybe when you're 50, you'll pull them out and listen to them! Those recordings are very interesting when you go back and listen to them many years later.
Maybe. My father was a very enthusiastic chronicler of my musical education. I'm sure he knows where they are. They're behind lock and key somewhere. I'm probably even now at the point where I'd find them entertaining. Ten years ago I would have happily lost those tapes.

Was it with Brancart, when you were 12 and 13, that you began to realize that playing the piano was becoming quite serious for yourself?
Yes, it's difficult to put a number on it, but I do remember when I was 13 I played with an orchestra for the first time. There was something about that experience and the thrill that it was to be on the stage that cemented certain things. I remember thinking, "Yes, this is it for me." It's not that earlier I had any ambivalence, I don't think. Because I certainly remember being passionate about music long before that. I remember, for example, when I was probably seven or eight my parents played a chamber music concert at the university. It was mostly the Brahms Clarinet Quintet, and it really made a huge impression on me. I remember being obsessed with those pieces, and I remember when I

went to school there were pieces we would listen to in the car. For example, there was Murray Perahia's recording of Mozart's K. 482, the Concerto in E-flat, and there was a recording of Serkin playing Beethoven's *Appassionata* Sonata. I remember insisting on listening to these pieces so much that the tape wore out! I remember those old cassettes. So my passion for music started very early. It was probably in my early teens when it started to occur to me that music wasn't something that would just always be in my life, but that it might be a career. I somehow always knew that it was my passion, but for a long time I didn't translate it into any kind of practical terms until a little bit later.

At about the age of 12 through 14, about how many hours were you devoting seriously to working at the piano?
I think it was probably in the area of three or maybe four, tops. I was never one for hugely long hours of practice, and I still am not. My teacher also didn't believe in it. She believed in less time and more concentrated work. I still think that is much better. There have been times in my life when I had so much repertoire to play that I was sitting at the piano six or seven hours a day. But I don't think it's healthy—mentally, physically, and probably above all, it's not good for one's relationship with music. I think eventually your emotional receptivity to the music starts to diminish when you're too immersed physically. I would say that when I was young, it was probably around three or four hours a day. When I say it, I know it is probably a lot less than some do, but it still sounds like plenty for me.

Would you characterize yourself as a very quick learner?
I think I'm medium. I think I have good ears and am a fairly good sight reader. I like a lot of time with a piece before I feel comfortable with it. Still now, my policy is that I don't play pieces after first learning them. I always learn them, leave them, and come back. I think that in terms of getting pieces into my fingers I'm fairly quick, but I find that there's a sense in which there is no substitute for time in terms of developing a comfort level with a piece of music. That's not new. I felt that way years ago.

Do you find that after you learn a piece and put it away and finally return to it that you change basic things like the fingering?
Practically, I think you hear differently. Things do change. For me, talking about technical issues like fingering, I find that everything is based in the ear. What we hear necessitates the physical, technical aspects. Yes, absolutely, it's amazing to me that you can spend hours a day with a piece of music you've worked with, and then sometimes if you leave it for a few months,

you find that the time away has, in a sense, done more. The instrument can sometimes be an obstacle, rather than a tool. Obviously I love the piano. It's my medium of choice, but it's a machine in some ways. It's not an especially natural implement for music making, surely not when compared with winds or strings in terms of their ability to produce a line. And particularly not in comparison with the human voice. Sometimes that's good to remember. If you sing a phrase, even if you're like me and you have no ability as a singer, it will reveal itself in more obvious ways rather than by hours of practicing.

You went to Leon Fleisher at Curtis when you were 17. You were with him for how many years?
Four years.

How did that opportunity come about?
For a few years before I went to him people were telling me that my next step should be to study with him. Many thought, including Brancart, that he would be the ideal teacher for me. I also grew up with his recordings, so for me it was kind of a dream scenario to get to go study with him. At one point—I can't remember if she was the one who set it up—I went to play for him when I was probably 13 or 14. So I developed a little bit of a relationship. Before I became a student of his, I had gone two or three times to play for him, so he was aware of me. He was on the faculty at Curtis, but when I went to audition, he wasn't actually there. But I knew that all of the faculty had to review the audition tapes. I had requested him as a teacher, and luckily enough, when I was accepted, I was assigned him as my teacher. It worked out exactly as I would have hoped.

Tell me about his teaching.
It's not easy to describe because it's very remarkable. What I always find myself saying about him is that he is the only person I know who is equally eloquent as a performer and as a speaker. Really the only one, without reservations, who I find is moving in both areas. And that's an amazing tool as a teacher. That meant that he was able to sit away from the piano and verbalize his ideas in a way which was incredibly exciting. He was incredibly able to offer a huge amount of information without the danger of his students wanting to imitate him because they were hearing so much. But then by the same token, sometimes you can talk—and I know this from my very limited experience teaching—until you're blue in the face, and you just need to play something for someone. Then he would sit down at the piano, and what he is able to produce at the piano is so remarkable that I really do feel that I

learned equal amounts from when he just sat and from having that sound in my ear all the time with what he was able to do with the instrument. In the few years I've had away from him, it doesn't seem any less remarkable.

This way of teaching—conjuring up images and talking, a prosaic word in this case—worked well with you, but there may be others who would become impatient and feel that they should be making more sound at the piano. You were working with him when he was not able to perform at all, is that correct?

Not exactly. I was working with him at the time his playing was coming back. I came to him in 1997, and if I'm correct it was 1995 when he played that first Mozart K. 414, Concerto in A Major, with the Boston Symphony at Tanglewood. Yes, it's been awhile. It seems like there has been a lot more publicity about it recently, but it's been on and off for over a decade now.

When he was teaching you during those four years, he was demonstrating with both hands equally well. Before that time, when he was teaching and not playing in public, was he able at all to demonstrate for students in the studio with both hands?

I remember when I first played for him, which would have been before he had started playing again with both hands (I'll never forget this!), I played Beethoven's op. 2, no. 3 in C major, and there was this difficult passage in the first movement which he played for me with one hand. I remember it because I couldn't believe what I was hearing. But I guess it does demonstrate that he was, more or less, just not able to play with the right hand. I never asked.

It was his right hand, but which finger?

His problems were, I think, with fingers three, four, and five. He'll be the first to say he's not cured. Even when you shake his hand, those three fingers are quite curled up, especially four and five. I think three is in much better shape than those two.

He went through Botox injections.

Amazing, isn't it? He has them periodically. He's open about it. It is a way around his dystonia. It is not something that has cured him for life.

When you started with Fleisher, what music were you playing?

I remember the first music I played for him was Mozart's K. 488, Concerto in A Major, and I remember that in that first semester, in 1997, I learned and played Schumann's *Davidsbündlertänze* for him.

So the *Davidsbündlertänze* have been with you a long time. I'm sure you still keep in close contact with him.
I do. I had the remarkable experience of getting to play with him this year. I played the Schumann concerto twice with him conducting in Japan. Wow! What an incredible week that was!

You made a comment in an earlier interview that you had experienced self-doubt while you were at Curtis. Do you remember making that remark?
Yes, that really made the rounds!

Looking back, philosophically, do you think self-doubt is a positive element for a performer?
Absolutely. What's really interesting about that interview[8] is that I really said all of those things. I wasn't misquoted. The guy who did the interview did a good job with it, actually. When I said those things I wasn't under the impression that I was saying anything that would be at all surprising, but it's been a frequent topic of conversation. For me, being a performing musician and playing and working with documents that are far greater than oneself—they're far greater than any performance of them could be—is intimidating. That is something that remains intimidating. I think that self-doubt is a very natural and healthy part of one's relationship with music.

I would think that if you don't have self-doubt something is wrong.
Absolutely. I also feel that if I had a criticism about the way that concert life is now, I think in a sense the existing system tends to reward invulnerability. I think that's wrong. I think one of the things that we find touching about the great performance is that there is vulnerability. There is doubt and there is something fragile. Don't misunderstand me. In order to go out there on the stage and play a piece, you have to have an incredibly clear view of what it is you want to say. And you have to have the confidence that an audience is going to sit there and listen to you. At the same time that always has to remain balanced against the feeling that whatever you're able to do that day, the piece could still be played so much better. That has nothing to do with self-doubt in relation to other performers because I think that is not ultimately what music is about. But that feeling that you're working toward something which is not really reachable is the most beautiful part, and maybe ultimately the most difficult, but at the same time the most ultimately rewarding aspect of what we do. Thinking about self-doubt, it was compounded by the fact that I had probably never been exposed to good pianists in that number that I was at Curtis. It was remarkable. There

were only 20 of us, but everyone played so well. That starts to play into your head a little bit!

But there are so many other factors, besides just being able to play well, that come into performing, wouldn't you say?
Oh, my God, absolutely! There are so many personality questions and there is so much luck involved.

Your physical health, for one.
Yes, I'm beginning to realize the extent to which one is able to live this life heavily lies on how well you take care of yourself. It seems so obvious but it was not something that occurred to me when I was younger.

Especially when you get to be 40 or 50.
I feel it already! When I'm eating healthy and going running, even if the flight was three hours late and I didn't have enough sleep, I'm able to find my energy level more easily than if I'm not taking care of myself.

You spoke a moment ago about your colleagues at Curtis in a general way. You've worked with Benjamin Hochman.[9] Was he at Curtis when you were there?
We came at exactly the same time. We've played together occasionally over the years, and most recently this year.

Would you care to mention any other of your contemporaries that might be of interest here?
Lang Lang came the same year that I did. Now that I look at it in retrospect, I think it's rather interesting that the three of us were there the same year. But there were any number of terrific pianists there.

Those have very likely gone on to become excellent teachers who are working in areas where they simply have not become household names. Changing the subject here, through your mother you got to know Isaac Stern when you were 15 and playing in Jerusalem. Stern is responsible for your earliest engagement with professional management. So you have had quite a different beginning from many pianists. You've never entered any competitions.
No, never. Yes, that was very lucky. Going back to Stern, I met him when I was quite young, and he was incredibly nice to me, and very enthusiastic. At that point, I was so far away from thinking about music in career terms,

as that had nothing to do with my relationship to music at that point. I was very flattered that he liked my playing, and that was basically all I thought about it. And then three months later, I had management, and I said, "How did this happen?" In a sense, I would wish everyone that kind of beginning to a career, rather than coming to a point when you have to think about how am I going to make a living and how is this going to happen. Instead, you're gifted your first break. All of a sudden I had management and I hadn't lifted a finger. I realize now I was so lucky. Oh, and by the way, management is not in any respect a guarantee of a career. But that set the ball rolling in a way that meant something that I never had to do. I can't tell you how much that pleases me.

You escaped all that stress and strain.
Yes, all that stress and strain focused in the wrong direction. I don't mind living the stress of performing. That seems very worthwhile. But the stress of going into a situation in front of a panel who is going to decide how you measured up is something that I can't think has in any way much to do with music.

Would you ever judge a competition yourself, or have you?
I haven't. I think I would be reluctant to do it. I know myself. I would get too nervous for all the performers and that I'd be a physical wreck. On top of that, there is something about the whole set of circumstances that would probably trouble me too much. I should never say never. When I think of all of the ways that one could potentially help young musicians, that is not the one that comes to mind, or that I'd want to be involved with.

You worked closely with Mitsuko Uchida during a European tour in the fall of 2004, after you were the recipient of a Borletti-Buitoni Trust Award in 2003. Is that her trust, or is she head of the trust?
No, she's not the head. She is one of an executive committee of four. But the trust was begun[10] very much because of her initiative. She's good friends with the Buitonis who, I think, single-handedly fund the trust. They are a wonderful Italian couple who run a concert series in Perugia, among other activities. Legend has it that Mitsuko was speaking with Ilaria, telling her that when performing artists are young and just starting out, it's very difficult for them because they worry a lot about money and about what they're going to do next year. Security is very far away. To which Ilaria said, "I have money. I should do something." This tells you a lot about what kind of people they are. They are incredibly generous and open.

Are they a middle-aged couple, or older?
Franco Buitoni is probably close to 70 and Ilaria Borletti is considerably younger. It's not Mitsuko's trust. She is the only one of the four who is a musician. In terms of musical values, it very much bears her stamp. It was her sense that there needed to be more advocacy for young musicians that the trust started. It has all of her fingerprints on it, in the absolute best sense.

How are you chosen?
People are asked to nominate young musicians, and when you're nominated you're approached and you're asked to put together a tape and a letter saying what the trust could do for you. Which is very smart. The trust doesn't give a cash prize. They ask you what you would do with the money, which is so smart.

In your case, what did you say?
I did a number of different things. First of all, I commissioned Lewis Spratlan's *Wonderer*,[11] which is something I probably would not have done at that point if I had had to pay for it. So this was wonderful. Since I was at the very beginning of my European career, the trust ended up paying a lot of travel expenses. I was at a point where I couldn't say I wouldn't do a concert just because it meant going over for just that one performance. So very often the trust would end up paying for me for four days, or whatever, across the Atlantic, which is something I try not to do anymore. It paid quite a lot of publicity expenses, which were very high at that point, and still are. Oh, yes, the biggest expense. I had always loved Curtis, but at the same time I felt sorry that I had never had an academic education. So the trust paid for me to take some classes at Columbia.

What did you study?
Over three semesters, I did a modern British literature class. I took a sociology class, and a political science course. I wish I were still doing it. But I ran into some time problems. There were always problems, but now it seems they are insurmountable. But I'm so happy I did it. And again, it is probably something I would have said to myself, "Yes, I'd love to, but it's so much money." I think the trust is such a wonderful organization. One of the trust's first winners was the Jerusalem Quartet. When they were asked what would you do with the money, they said, "We've been playing together full-time basically since we were children (they began when they were 13 or 14) and because playing has kept us so busy we're afraid we haven't widened our musical spheres. We want the trust to pay for us to take a sabbatical away from

each other so that we can go do other things." Which I think was incredibly rewarding for them. They refreshed and went and did other things. One person studied, because he had stopped when he was too young, and another played chamber music festivals with other musicians. That's the kind of organization the trust is. They work with you to see how they can help.

Would that we could find such people more often!
I don't think that generosity and wealth necessarily go together. This was just the perfect situation where things came together. Someone like Mitsuko, who identified the problem and someone who had the means to do something about it. You never know where it might pop up. There are a few people. Not many of them. I've been very lucky to have gotten awards. I've received a Gilmore and an Avery Fisher Career Grant, which are both wonderful, but I think that there is something about how the trust works that is so unique.

Richard Goode has also been one of your mentors, and you have a set of recitals coming up soon with him.
We're playing two concerts in London next May. Four hands, and two pianos.

What music will you be playing?
It's a wacky program, which I absolutely love. It begins with Schubert's *Lebensstürme* in A minor, D. 947, for four hands, which was written during the last year of his life. It's incredible, and I think not any less extraordinary than his *Fantasie*. We continue with a special favorite of mine, Schumann's *Six Canonic Études for the Pedal Piano*, which Debussy transcribed for two pianos because there are no pedal pianos anymore.[12] Then the program continues with Beethoven's *Grosse Fugue*, which he himself wrote for four hands. It is not a transcription. That's the first half! And then we have Stravinsky's *Agon*, for which, again, we have his own version for two pianos. It's not someone else's transcription.

Did he write that for rehearsal purposes?
I don't know. Richard has just sent me the score, and I haven't even looked at it yet. I do see that it involves the castanets. I don't know what it was prepared for, but it will be very interesting when I look into it. I love the piece. And then we end with Debussy's *En blanc et noir*. I love the program. It's really very interesting. Richard is, in addition to being an impossibly wonderful pianist, one of the most intelligent, inquisitive, and interested people I know.

I'm guessing that the rehearsal process is going to be exciting. For me—it seems like the wrong way around perhaps—collaboration is almost the more important part. It's the mutual exploration.

You have noted elsewhere that if you were not in music you would be doing something language related. Did you study languages?
I have studied languages. I speak French. Badly. And I'm learning German. But it wouldn't be something in languages. I would be involved in writing somehow. That's my second passion.

Nonfiction?
Yes, probably. I'm an avid reader of great novels, but I don't think that I have that kind of imagination. I'm not sure yet because it's a hypothetical.

I want to go back to your family. Usually interviews start with your family, and I'm always wondering when I'll read something about your background that doesn't mention your father's mother. But I suppose that's inevitable. And I'm sure you don't mind!
No, certainly not.

How well did you know your grandmother Raya Garbousova?
On the one hand, very well because I was 16 when she died. She lived a few hours' drive away from us, so I remember her very well and have affectionate memories of her. She was, in addition to being a great cellist, a very doting grandmother. Grandchildren for her at that point in her life were the most important thing, and she found it very exciting that there was a budding musician in the family. But at the same time, she had carpel tunnel surgery the year I was born. I have no memory of her as a cellist and I don't think I ever saw her hold the instrument, which is sad. Even though I knew she had been a great cellist and she had had a distinguished past, I think that somehow I wasn't really aware of the extent of it when I was growing up. I remember that at her memorial service there were some recordings played which I think that my father and my uncle had chosen. I sat up and thought, "She was really unbelievable." In a sense, now that it is too late, it makes me sad. I really didn't know her on a musical level.

So you didn't know her well enough on that level to talk with her about her past?
Well, I think she probably wasn't that interested in living in the past. And I don't think I realized that she was such a gold mine. Now, of course, I would

be dying to know what it was like to play with Heifetz and Rubinstein and all of those people she played with. Maybe there is a downside to living in the kind of musical household I grew up in. It all seemed very normal to me. Take Isaac Stern, for example. I only seriously met him when I was 16, but he was in the house a couple of times and I didn't think anything of it. There were so many musicians of that caliber. Basically there was a great lesson, you know. I was very comfortable around those musicians.

Tell me about your mother.
She was born in Romania, but the family moved to Israel when she was two. Her mother is still there and her family. I go back to visit more or less every year.

You've played chamber music with your mother, Miriam Fried, from your earliest years. Do you remember your earliest professional performances with her? How old were you and what did you play?
I was 13 when we played the Dvořák *Sonatina*.

You mentioned playing your first concerto when you were 13. Would that have been under your father's conducting?
No, it wasn't. I said that I never entered competitions, and that's not quite true. I did when I was little. I played with the Bloomington Symphony. It was a civic orchestra that had no connection with the university. I would say that it was a semiprofessional orchestra.

I did wonder how that worked with your father, Paul Biss, being a conductor at the school and how that would work with the son of the orchestra conductor.
That would have been far too embarrassing. I did come back once, and that would have been after I had been away and had a certain reputation that was far removed from being a student. That would have been very bad for my father. When I was 16 I did win the school's concerto competition, which meant I ended up playing with the orchestra as the winner of the competition, and that was only in my capacity as a student. Even then, I felt a little bit uncomfortable about it. My father was not conducting. If he had been, I wouldn't have entered. I was always very conscious of the fact that it was a big blessing for me growing up in a household like that and I didn't want personally to feel that I was taking advantage of it, and I didn't want anyone else to sense that.

What pianists do you remember hearing play when you were growing up in Bloomington? Surely the university had a good concert series.
Amazingly, not. There is almost no tradition of guest artists in Bloomington. I think it's because there is such an incredible wealth of musical events at the university that they didn't need guest artists.

Really? The University of Iowa did when I was there. And I know that the University of Illinois did. Students need a chance to hear great artists who are out in the world playing.
Oh, absolutely. I know that when I went to play at Oberlin they had a series of guest concerts. Of course, there were Menahem Pressler and György Sebok who played from time to time. I don't remember that a great pianist ever came through Bloomington. Maybe I'm forgetting something. I really doubt it!

I'm sure if they were there, you would have heard them.
Oh, absolutely. I think occasionally we went to Indianapolis to hear the orchestra. And my grandparents lived in Illinois so I also grew up going to the Chicago Symphony concerts.

Who did you hear in Chicago when you were growing up? Who was important for you?
I remember I heard Leon Fleisher in a one-handed recital, and I heard him play the Ravel Left-Hand Concerto. I remember hearing Murray Perahia, and that was a wonderful, memorable concert. I remember hearing András Schiff play a recital in Orchestra Hall. I remember hearing Peter Serkin play. I remember hearing Yefim Bronfman play, and that was actually in Bloomington. He and Stern came and played a recital together, and in fact that was the first time I met Mr. Stern. But that's the only case I can remember of people of that caliber coming to town. There is a series, but they have maybe one classical concert a year. It's theater acts and things like that.

What instrument did you play on when you were growing up at home?
I was very lucky. The very first few years there was just an upright in our house, but I think I was about 10 when my parents bought a Steinway Hamburg B, which is actually my piano now. They have since moved to Boston and are living in an apartment, and they decided they didn't need the piano anymore, especially since my mother has a piano in her studio in the New England Conservatory. So she has access to a piano whenever she wants it.

So now, after many years of not having played it, it's my piano again and I have it here in my apartment in New York.

Are you familiar with the new Italian Fazioli?
I've played a couple, which I was not bowled over by, but I will keep trying them.

What about the Australian Stuart instrument?
That I'm not familiar with.

Do you think that you will be a teacher yourself one day?
Oh, yes. I love the very limited amount of teaching that I've done. I think it's an incredible learning experience for the teacher as well. I would just have to have a little more stability in my life for that. With the amount of traveling I'm doing now, it isn't possible.

You have a lot of time for that yet.
I hope so.

You've played at the Risor Chamber Music Festival on the coast of Norway. What are the audiences like there?
The audiences are amazing. I think it has something to do with the fact that Leif Ove Andsnes is the director. He's widely admired around the world, and especially in Norway. It's the kind of festival where there are four or five concerts a day and every one of them is completely packed in this smallish church. It's amazing how many people they fit into that church! It's a wonderful atmosphere there. Risor is a fishing village which is very, very beautiful. One doesn't sleep because there are so many concerts and rehearsals, but also because the sun never goes down. I loved being there. It was extremely concentrated, but I enjoyed the work and the performances very much. Everybody who goes there seems to love it. There were a lot of different people there: the press, and people who had organized trips around it. Everybody has a good time. There is a tremendous amount of goodwill in the air at the festival.

Thinking again about particular audiences, do you have any memorable anecdotes about experiences with audiences during a performance?
Yes, I do. There is one that springs to mind, although I'm sure in the next days I'll think of more of them. I played a chamber music concert which

was quite remarkable as there was a problem with the stage lights. They had not functioned during the first piece. So the stage crew found a collection of lamps for us, because it was a really dark room. These lamps were going to give us just enough light to see. But there was a problem with finding a position with the lamps which lit our music but didn't bring an impossible glare into the audience's eyes. So I remember there was a lot of back and forth about it, and we ended up in the first half where we were in a position where we couldn't see. When we walked on stage for the second half for the Brahms Horn Trio, the horn player said he couldn't see at all. Since I was closest to the light, I was the one who got up to adjust them. And 150 people got up and started screaming at me. It was horrible. The whole audience was screaming that the light was in their eyes. And I don't remember that we found a particularly good solution. But we were the people in the dark in the end. It was really hard to sit back down and feel motivated to play after that. It was not exactly an easy situation for us either.

Let's talk about your recording contemporary composers you have played. We've mentioned Lewis Spratlan, and you've played Leon Kirchner. Do you have any plans to record their music?
Not at the moment. One thing that I'm very happy about is a performance I played—not the world premiere but the American premiere—of the Kirchner piece that was written for me and has now been released on a CD of his music on Albany Records. I'm very happy about this recording. But right now I'm recording with EMI, which is basically a wonderful blessing, but given the state of the classical-music recording industry they do have to be careful about what they record. So I think recording contemporary music is not without its complications. At the same time, I would say that recording is an outgrowth of performance. It's not the starting point. The important thing is that you play that music. Obviously I'm going to continue to play contemporary music. At some point I'm sure the timing will be right and I'll chose the pieces which are most important, and find a way to record them.

You will. Eventually. This spring you recorded four Beethoven sonatas and I understand that they are being released in the fall of this year. What do you plan next for EMI?
It's not 100 percent finalized but it should be a Mozart concerto release. It works really well because if I think about the composers who loom largest in my life I would say Mozart, Beethoven, and Schumann. Then they will all be represented in my first three records. So that's the plan.

And what orchestra?
That's not 100 percent firm yet.

You're playing three Mozart concertos[13] next Sunday in Chicago with James Conlon and the Chicago Symphony Orchestra. I caught you today as you are getting those back into your mind.
Yes. I've never played three concertos in one day.

It seems to be becoming something of the norm now, you know. Pierre-Laurent Aimard played three concertos in St. Paul with the Saint Paul Chamber Orchestra in early June. Not three Mozart concertos, but he did start out with an early Mozart C major concerto.
Number eight.

Yes, exactly. He conducted it from the keyboard. Then he played the Ligeti concerto, which, of course, is in his blood. After intermission he played the Ravel G Major, which I'm sure he's played at least a dozen times.
He did not conduct that from the keyboard, did he?

No, he did not conduct the Ligeti and he did not conduct the Ravel.
That would be a little much, I would think!

Douglas Boyd, the Scottish conductor, did the honors. Wonderful programming and very exciting.
You can see so many sides to his personality that way. My God.

I want to change the subject here drastically, and return to thinking about Schumann again, as he is central to your musical passions, especially his *Kreisleriana* and the *Fantasie*. Which recordings of his major works did you listen to when you were younger?
With those pieces, Cortot was certainly someone I listened to as I was growing up. I loved those recordings. There is a recording of Murray Perahia which is, I think, the first *Davidsbündlertänze* I ever heard. That is wonderful. For Schumann's concerto I remember the recording that Dinu Lipatti made. That's probably the one that I loved the most. Recently I've listened to Schnabel, who is someone you wouldn't readily associate with that piece, but it's magnificent. It's a live performance with the New York Philharmonic. Those were some of the firsts. Cortot certainly in all of the big solo pieces.

Do you play Chopin at all?
Oh, absolutely. I've played a lot of him. It's just a coincidence that I haven't for the last couple of years, but I will certainly come back to him. I adore Chopin, and he was one of my first musical loves and remains so.

Do you compose at all?
I don't. It would be wonderful to compose, but it's something that I don't have any particular ability for. The extent of my composing is that when I play Mozart concertos I write the cadenzas when I need to. It's an incredibly useful exercise.

How about the ones you are playing next week?
Actually, no. K. 456 and K. 459 have cadenzas. The one exception is the D Minor, K. 466, for which Beethoven wrote a long cadenza for this rondo. For this movement I wrote my own because I find that even as great as Beethoven's cadenza is, it is slightly inappropriate. It's very long and doesn't fit the piece. This may be impertinent for me to say, but I don't like it. Beethoven's first movement cadenza for the D Minor is already not especially idiomatic. It really sounds more like Beethoven than Mozart, but it is so compelling and so wonderful and quite in keeping with the spirit of the piece I couldn't not play it. On the other hand, the cadenza that Beethoven wrote for the last movement is wonderful as a piece of music, but not appropriate there if you look at the kind of cadenzas that Mozart wrote for his own rondos. But then I ended up writing something that is about 45 seconds. So in this concert there will be very little by me.

What do you do to keep yourself energized for the job of playing?
It's difficult. I try to do some physical exercise every day. When I can possibly find the time, I go running every day. For me it provides incredible energy. I am very careful about what I eat and when I eat. But still, I've just had my annual month off and I'm in much better shape. It's very, very difficult to maintain when you're traveling, but you do the best you can just thinking about what your body needs to feel that you're in charge of it and trying to do as much of that as possible.

Do you have any preconcert rituals?
I try whenever I can to take a nap in the afternoon and to have some quiet time. It's not always possible. As for eating, I just try to regulate how many hours before the concert I eat. Trying to find the balance between eating

enough so that I'm not hungry, and yet not eating too much and feeling full. I don't have any rituals.

And you're able to handle nerves fairly well?
Yes. It's a natural part of performing. If I'm not nervous on stage, I would think the concert doesn't mean enough to me. But it's not something I feel uneasy about.

I want to thank you so much for sharing your time. You have shared your thoughts that others will hopefully be interested in hearing.
I hope so.

Select Discography

Franz Schubert. Piano Sonata in C Major, D. 840, *Reliquie*; Sonata in A Major, D. 959. György Kurtág. "Birthday elegy for Judit—for the second finger of her left hand" (from *Játékok*); *Spoken Introduction*; "Hommage à Schubert" (from *Játékok*). Recorded live at Wigmore Hall. 2009.

W. A. Mozart. Piano Concerto in C Major, K. 467; Piano Concerto in E-flat Major, K. 482. Orpheus Chamber Orchestra. Recorded in concert. EMI Classics 50999 2 17270 23. 2008.

Ludwig van Beethoven. Sonatas: # 8 in C Minor, op. 13, *Pathétique*; # 15 in D Major, op. 28, *Pastoral*; # 27 in E Minor, op. 90; # 30 in E Major, op. 109. EMI Classics 0946 3 944 22 25. 2007.

Leon Kirchner. Works for Solo Piano. Piano Sonata # 1 (1948), Leon Fleisher; *Interlude I* (1989), Peter Serkin; *Five Pieces for Piano* (1987), Max Levinson; *Interlude II* (2002), Jonathan Biss; *The Forbidden* (2006), Joel Fan; Sonata # 2 (2002), Jeremy Denk. Albany, Troy 906. 2007.

Robert Schumann. *Fantasie* in C Major, op. 17; *Kreisleriana*, op. 16; *Arabeske* in C Major, op. 18. EMI Classics 0946 3 65391 2. 2007.

Ludwig van Beethoven. *Fantasy* in G Minor, op. 77; Robert Schumann. *Davidsbündlertänze*, op. 6; Beethoven. Piano Sonata in F Minor, op. 57, *Appassionata*. EMI Debut Series 5 85894 2. 2004.

Notes

1. See Introduction for details about Leon Fleisher.

2. Kirchner (b. 1919); Spratlan (b. 1940); Takemitsu (1930–1996); Rhim (b. 1952); Corigliano (b. 1938); Danielpour (b. 1956); Ludwig (b. 1974).

3. Anthony Tommasini, "Pianist at Last Has Carnegie Hall to Himself," *The New York Times*, 23 Jan. 2011.

4. Daniel Biss took math degrees at Harvard and MIT, later joining the math faculty at the University of Chicago. He gave up his teaching post, and now represents Chicago's northern suburbs in the Illinois House of Representatives as a Democrat.

5. Andrew Mays won the Cliburn Foundation's fifth International Piano Competition for Outstanding Amateurs in Fort Worth, Texas, in June 2007. As an ophthalmologist he serves as residency program director for the Department of Ophthalmology at the University of Alabama at Birmingham, and is on the staff at the VA Medical Center in Birmingham, Alabama.

6. Karen Taylor is director of Indiana University's Jacobs School of Music Piano Academy and the Young Pianists Program.

7. Evelyne Brancart is chair of the Department of Piano at Indiana University. Following her earliest studies at the Brussels Conservatory, she studied with Leon Fleisher.

8. Jeremy Eichler, "Young Pianist at the Ready to Believe in His Success," *The New York Times*, 8 Mar. 2005.

9. Benjamin Hochman (b. 1980 in Jerusalem) studied with Richard Goode at Mannes and Claude Frank at Curtis. Biss and Hochman played a program of music for four hands, two pianos in November of 2006 at the 92nd St. Y in New York City.

10. The Borletti-Buitoni Trust was established in 2002 and is based in London.

11. Spratlan wrote *Wonderer* in 2005 for Biss who premiered it in Portland, Maine, in February of 2006.

12. Biss played the Schumann with Hochman in November of 2006 at the 92nd St. Y in New York City.

13. Mozart's B-flat Major, K. 456; F Major, K. 459; and D Minor, K. 466; at the Ravinia Pavilion, 8 July 2007.

Simone Dinnerstein. Photo by Raphael Stein

CHAPTER THREE

~

Simone Dinnerstein

Simone Dinnerstein was born in Brooklyn, New York, on the 18th of September in 1972 after her parents returned from her father's Fulbright year in Germany. Both parents had a profound artistic, although not directly musical, influence on their daughter. Today Dinnerstein continues to make Brooklyn her home, with her husband, Jeremy Greensmith, and their son, Adrian. Greensmith teaches at Brooklyn's PS 321, where their son is a student and Dinnerstein herself has made artistic commitments.

Although it was in London that the 15-year-old Dinnerstein first met her future husband, he was not the reason she spent her first summer there. She was there to study with the preeminent teacher Maria Curcio[1] who had settled in London in the mid-1960s and became legendary for her work with many pianists. Today Dinnerstein credits her father's vision for her study with Curcio and reveals in our interview how Curcio began her piano instruction. She mentions several pianists who had earlier worked with Curcio, but among those she did not mention were Leon Fleisher, himself an excellent teacher; Radu Lupu; and Martha Argerich. One finds a connection to Curcio's influential teaching in the background of numerous prominent pianists today.

Maria Curcio was a diminutive figure who began her life as a pianist at a very young age in Naples, where she was born into an affluent environment to a Brazilian-Jewish mother and an Italian father. Because her mother was a pianist, her daughter found excellent instruction. Curcio was only 15 when she became a pupil of Artur Schnabel in Lake Como in the late 1930s, and made her name after her London debut in 1939. Her performances in

Amsterdam brought her into further contact with Schnabel and with his personal secretary, Peter Diamand, her future husband. Curcio followed Diamand to Amsterdam when he became director of the Holland Festival. World War II, however, caught up with him. Because they were Jewish, he and his mother were forced into hiding, and it was Curcio who kept them alive. The privations and stress of the war years caused Curcio great physical suffering, as she became malnourished and later developed tuberculosis. She was brought to the point of not being able to walk. Many years were spent away from the piano, and only slowly did she regain her physical abilities after years of struggle. She married Diamand after the war, and in 1965 they went to Edinburgh where he began his directorship of the Edinburgh Festival. She had already come into contact with many prominent English musicians, most notably Benjamin Britten, who was a great encouragement for her return to playing, which she did for a brief period. She played frequently with Britten, and appeared in chamber music performances with other prominent musicians of the day. By 1963 she had given her last public solo recital. She was by this time recognized for her teaching and for several years held a visiting-professor post at the Royal Academy of Music. But it was within her home that she later developed her most loyal followers, including Dinnerstein.

Bach's *Goldberg Variations* have played a central role in Dinnerstein's musical life. In 2005 she made her New York debut at Weill Recital Hall with the piece, and in 2007 she came to the musical world's attention with the release of her recording of the work. Earlier she had raised funds to record the work herself. She promptly sent it to numerous recording labels to find one with an interest in releasing it. Telarc took the chance on releasing her recording, which quickly garnered enthusiastic praise. Her story about learning the piece became legendary. When she discovered she was expecting her first child she decided it was time to learn this landmark of keyboard literature, and thus began her musical journey with Bach along with her personal journey toward motherhood.

The energetic Dinnerstein does not lack initiative or fresh ideas, many of which, one hopes, will not wither by the restraints of her time. Hers is a distinct voice for the contemporary composer. In addition, she believes strongly that many different musical genres should join hands with mainstream classical music to invite more involvement from those who do not come readily to classical music. For example, she performed in February 2010 with Kristian Järvi's Absolute Ensemble at Le Poisson Rouge in its program "Absolute Bach Re-invented." She offered Gene Pritsker's *Reinventions*, a Bach-like collage. Järvi's Absolute Ensemble meshes together performers from jazz, rock, world music, and hip-hop.

At the piano Dinnerstein presents a quietly understated presence. One senses no playing to the gallery from her. Her Bach performances are stately. She performs Schubert's op. 90 Impromptus as intimate, cozy *Hausmusik*, overlooking the fact that she is playing a modern nine-foot instrument in a large hall. Her whisper can make a deeper impression than any roar. Her recital programs are chosen with care, showing a thread that clearly connects one piece directly to another.

I sat down with Dinnerstein on the 5th of December in 2009 for conversation the morning after her recital in Madison, Wisconsin, at the University's Union Theatre. We began by speaking about her father, the painter Simon Dinnerstein, who spent the year before her birth in 1971–1972 on a Fulbright award studying at the Hochschule für Bildende Kunste in Kassel, Germany. At that time he began his large oil-on-wood painting *The Fulbright Triptych* (1971–1974) which documents in photographic detail his living and working environment during that year. While in Germany, he completed most of the large central panel, showing his main living area and studio as well as the views from the two windows. His wife is seated, wearing a plaid skirt in the left panel. After returning to Brooklyn, he spent three years working on the triptych. In the completed work, he appears seated in the right panel, and his infant daughter, Simone, is seated on her mother's lap. Today the triptych is part of the permanent collection of the Palmer Museum of Art at Pennsylvania State University, and is reproduced in the liner notes of Simone's 2011 Sony recording *Bach: A Strange Beauty*.

Interview

Your father is a living example of the importance of art in life.
Yes, art was the thing of the highest value in our family. Both of my parents are interested in art. Even though my mother is not an artist, it's very important to her, too. She was a very creative and highly imaginative teacher as an early-childhood educator, and is now working as a consultant helping teachers. She was always very child centered, and that also affected me because of how she raised me and also because of her commitment to her field of work. Both of my parents are very idealistic people who have passion for what they do. It's very important for them to do what you're doing as well as you can. Not to just succeed in a kind of commercial way but to succeed in the sense of doing what you intended to do to the best of your ability. When we traveled it was always to see art. We never took nature trips. I became more interested in nature trips and hiking only after I met my husband.

You lived in Rome when you were quite young during the time your father had a Rome Prize Fellowship at the American Academy from 1976 to 1978. Do you remember living there?

Yes, very much. I was in Rome this past spring, and actually found our apartment building while walking in the neighborhood where we lived. I recognized it, because it made a very strong impression on me. I also remember very well the art that I saw in Rome. The general culture and values there made a huge impression on me when I was young. I remember very clearly that when I returned to Brooklyn, I was shocked because it was such a place of pop culture. I didn't grow up with television at all. I grew up wearing long skirts, because the Italian girls wore long skirts, and beautiful clothes. Now I think Italy is more similar to the United States.

You began ballet lessons in Rome, and at those lessons you developed the desire to learn to play the piano.

Yes, that was another difference from the States. There was a pianist who played for the class and I asked my parents whether I could learn to play. My parents didn't have any background in music, so my father talked to one of the composers at the American Academy about a teacher. He suggested that I start with recorder lessons, and my father found an American recorder teacher who gave me lessons there in Rome. My parents were friends with members of the group Calliope, so my first introduction to music was through playing and listening to Renaissance music.

When you returned to Brooklyn from Rome, who was your teacher?

I started lessons when I was seven with a wonderful teacher, Linda Boppert, who had trained at music school. I studied with her for two years. I think she was overwhelmed by my response to the whole thing, because I was so excited about playing. Later on, she told my parents that I was actually one of her first students. She thought that everybody was going to be like this. I remember really enjoying dictation with her, writing down a melody when she played it. I loved doing that. In retrospect it seems like such a nerdy thing to have enjoyed as a seven-year-old! After I studied with her, by the age of nine my parents realized I should have a very serious, experienced teacher. Through friends, they found Solomon Mikowsky,[2] who became my main teacher until I graduated from high school.

What was Mikowsky's teaching like?

He was very methodical, giving me certain exercises such as scales, arpeggios, Hanon, Czerny, and Moszkowski's études. He was very deliberate about the pieces he chose for me to play. I would learn a certain group, which turned out to be basically a recital program each year, and there was much sight reading as well with him. In my earliest years I was doing simpler Beethoven, Mozart, and some of Chopin's nocturnes. He was extremely careful about the repertoire he gave me to learn. After studying with him I went to study with Maria Curcio in London. She was the opposite in that she gave me a new piece of music to learn for each lesson. She was very, very demanding, as she gave me music that was out of my reach. Her approach was the opposite from that of Mikowsky as she wanted to stretch me to try things I didn't feel I could do. Then when I went to Peter Serkin,[3] I had to bring in a new piece, memorized, to each lesson, so it was even more of a stretch.

Tell me how you came to study with Curcio.
My father read an article about her. She had taught Barry Douglas and José Feghali and this article appeared right after they had won the competitions.[4] I was going on a trip with my school chorus to London, so I auditioned for her while there. She was very different from anyone I had met before and completely different from Dr. Mikowsky, who, for one thing, was much younger than she was. She was in her late 70s and had studied with Schnabel. And she came from a very different, even mystical, world. When she played, her touch sounded like it came from a different time. It was really unusual. At the same time it was a sound that I wanted and that I had been looking for. I couldn't quite find how to do it. Then she also had a very different idea about technique in that she didn't separate it as much from the music. She made it all one thing. The technique was to bring the music to life and therefore they were much more connected. It was less a feeling of facility, but rather about how technique related to how you approach the instrument and how you draw the sounds out of that instrument. She had a very particular way of doing that. She spent the first six months changing the way I held my hands and giving me a different kind of awareness of my whole body and how it functioned when I play the piano. So in the end, putting together Dr. Mikowsky's approach and Maria's and Peter's was actually a great triad of teachers for me.

Did she free up your body more, perhaps using yoga?
Yes, she was interested in Alexander Technique and yoga. She started by changing the way I use my hands. I used to play with a very flat hand and lift my fingers up high. She wanted me to have a curved hand and have what she called a bridge of my hand, which meant my knuckles were to be higher. She wanted me to look like I was holding an orange in my hand. She worked with me to increase the independence of my fingers from each other and to be aware of the fact that my fingers could be extremely strong but that didn't need to affect my wrist. My wrist could be loose and my arms could be loose.

Her method was dividing each section of my body so it started with the fingers, then went to the wrist, and to the triceps, then to my back, my stomach, and down to my feet. Each being part of what I was doing. And she had a very particular way of doing this. When I first started studying with her she had me sitting on an extremely low bench where I was lower than the keys so that I could see how my fingers worked on their own. Then as I started to understand that, and how they could do something separate from the other part of my body, then I started to raise the bench. It's an interesting way of doing it because it's easy to think that your arms propel what you're doing, and if you know it's coming from your fingers, then you can add in your arm or take away your arm. You can add weight or take away weight. She made it very clear to me in a very tactile way how it worked. Before I studied with her, I used to move around a lot when I played. I was very emotive and would hunch my shoulders. She taught me that being still when I played actually made it possible for me to be much more expressive, to have a lot more power, and just be more focused. Now I don't really move that much and I'm much more relaxed.

You were quite young when you went to her but at the same time you had already had a lot of earlier training. Was it difficult to change your habits?
Oh, it was very hard. I started when I was 15, in the summertime. I went to her for three summers, and later I moved to London. For the first six months that I lived there she was incredibly tough on me. As I said, I had to bring in a different piece, which was new to me, for each lesson. We did loads of exercises, for example, Clementi and Brahms exercises. She was very tough, not giving an inch! It was very hard for me. Some people were really destroyed by her because she was so bruising to them. What I realized was that the way she taught was that you had to become her. Then after studying with her, you really had to reject her. But it was actually interesting because I can almost always tell a pianist who has studied with her because they do have such a strong imprint of her in their playing. It's a really good thing, but then you discover who you are and what your own values are. I think now that perhaps she wouldn't like everything I do in my playing, but she would be able to tell that I took a great deal from her. She taught Mitsuko Uchida and Pierre-Laurent Aimard. Christopher Taylor, who teaches here in Madison, also studied with her.

What was her teaching schedule like?
Curcio taught three lessons a day and each was about two hours long. She didn't watch the clock. Lessons started with espresso while sitting in a very dark room talking about many different things. I saw her twice a week, and she was extremely helpful to me in adjusting her rates for the lessons. I had a spon-

sor who had paid for me to be able to study with her in the first place. Without my sponsor and her giving me a break, I wouldn't have been able to do it.

After returning to New York, you worked with Serkin at Juilliard. Was this once a week?
No, it was not once a week because he was often out of town. I probably had two or three lessons a month and each lesson was about two hours long. I really had to know the music, because he would take the music and sit at the other end of the room during the lesson. During a lot of the lesson I didn't have the music in front of me. I had to know not only the notes, but all the markings, all of which were very meaningful for him. His way of teaching made me take in things very deeply and quickly. I think he was a great person for me to study with after Maria because he was so idiosyncratic. While he really respected tradition and fully knew the tradition of playing a certain piece, it was almost like he was trying to understand the music for the first time when he taught. We covered a little of Mozart's works and with Beethoven we covered a few sonatas and a few concertos. I tried to bring a new Bach prelude and fugue, memorized, to each lesson. With Serkin, it was Schumann, Schubert, and mostly the core repertoire. I actually didn't do much contemporary music with him at all. My taste in contemporary music is quite different from his. He felt it was very important to play contemporary music but to play the music you feel an affinity toward. I wasn't on the same page with him, in terms of his taste, but I did study Messiaen's *Quartet for the End of Time* with him, which was great.

Do you play other Messiaen pieces? Serkin is known for his recording of the *Vingt regards*.
I have played the Variations for Violin and Piano and haven't yet played the *Vingt regards* but would love to.

When you were about 12, 13, or 14, do you remember about how many hours a day you devoted to practicing at the piano?
It was probably about three or maybe four hours, but I didn't like practicing when I was growing up. It was a real struggle for me to practice because it just wasn't interesting to me. The music was always interesting to me, but I didn't want to practice it. It was hard for me to practice three hours, and of course I was doing it completely independently, because my parents weren't involved with my practicing at any point. Not any time from when I started. Which is interesting to me today because I've tried having my son learn, but I have to sit with him when he practices or he won't do it. Or he doesn't know how to do it. So many friends of mine grew up with their parents helping them with their practicing, either by sitting with them, or checking in on them.

My parents wouldn't have known whether I was doing it right or wrong. So it was really rather hard to practice. Very few young students have that kind of concentration and focus. But when I went to college, at about age 16, I started to practice a lot and to understand the value of practice at the piano.

When you were in London who did you hear play?
I saw a fabulous recital by Annie Fischer, who was a friend of Maria's. She was one of Maria's pianists, among those she admired. It was Fischer's last recital in London.[5] Dr. Mikowsky's favorite pianist was Shura Cherkassky,[6] a very different kind of pianist, but a fabulous pianist, too. He was more pianistic, that is, he was interested in sheer pianism—you know, the imagination of being a pianist. Although she certainly was a great pianist, Annie Fischer was more interested in being a musician than in being a pianist. So there are, you know, many different ways of getting to the music. I also saw Ivo Pogorelich,[7] whom I've always loved and think is an incredible pianist. The recital of his that I remember the most was the first time I heard him in Carnegie Hall when he played *Gaspard de la nuit* and Prokofiev's Sixth Sonata. It was great. I heard some recitals of Daniel Barenboim that were interesting to me. But when I was a teenager the person I was most inspired by was Mitsuko Uchida. I heard all of her concerts in New York and really looked up to her. I was a huge Glenn Gould fan, but, of course, I never saw him perform. I first heard his *Goldberg Variations*—his second recording—when I was 13. A friend of mine played it for me. It was amazing. Actually that was the first CD I had when I got my first CD player. I got Gould's *Goldberg Variations* and Bob Dylan [*laughs*]. When I was 15, in London, I first met my husband who was even more obsessed with Gould than I was. He had almost every recording that Gould had ever done. I listened to all of them. When I was about 14 or 15 there was a film festival of Glenn Gould at the Metropolitan Museum and I spent two days—seven hours each day—watching the films of him. There is just nobody like him. He's so imaginative. This creativity was just coming out of him.

Were there others you gravitated toward?
Once I started studying with Maria I got very interested in both Schnabel and Cortot and started collecting their recordings and I really loved them. Now I'm really fascinated by Myra Hess[8] and have started collecting her recordings.

What in particular is there about her playing that intrigues you?
I first started listening to her because a few friends said that my playing reminded them of her. It was very eerie because when I listened to her I felt that there is something about her playing that is very similar to how I feel.

Can you describe exactly what that is?
There is a kind of flexibility to her rhythm, her way of speaking the music. It's very shaped, free, and feels spoken to me—almost like a narrative. When I say free, there is not total freedom, of course, because she's not just doing whatever she wants. But there's a freshness in how she's interpreting the music, and in the moment of how she's playing. Her touch is just so beautiful.

And her tempo?
She tends to play things slower, and I play things slower, too. I find it easier to hear when I play slower and when I hear others play slower, and so possibly she felt that way. I know that she became friendly with the duo-pianists, the Contiguglia brothers,[9] who studied with her. They've talked with me about their lessons with her and apparently she thought everybody played too fast. So, yes, there is a lot in common with her.

After graduating from Juilliard in 1996, you played under the auspices of the Piatigorsky Foundation for several years.
Yes, I auditioned for them after I graduated. They had a small roster of artists that they would send out on tours. You would usually do a 10-day tour in a very specific location like northern Louisiana or east Texas and you'd play every day in a different town in community centers, nursing homes, and lots of churches. The concert would be an hour long and you'd talk about the music as well. It was a really fabulous experience for me. The experience of being on a tour, meeting all those people and being in places I would never have been in and having to really communicate the music was a huge learning curve for me. It wasn't just the playing, but it was also about how I talked about the music to interest people to have a good experience with unfamiliar music. All of these things really helped me grow a lot.

I want to change the subject here and ask you about a different aspect of being an artist. What are your thoughts about self-doubt, which is an inevitable part of life?
This is a difficult thing to talk about! For me, I'm always questioning how I'm playing and whether I'm doing justice to the music. As far as my career, I always knew that music was going to be a part of my life. I knew from when I started music that there was not going to be anything else. I knew from the beginning.

How do you keep the music that you play so frequently completely fresh for each time that you approach playing it for an audience?

Actually, one of the things is knowing that I'm playing in a different hall and on a different piano. Every piano has its own peculiarities and every hall has its own acoustic. Doing it on a different piano in a different hall makes it feel like it's a new piece in a way because it brings out different qualities of the music. Some pianos can't do certain articulations that I want to do, so it forces me to play differently. As far as freshness is concerned, I've talked to actors about this. I have a friend who is a fabulous actor who does long runs of shows, performing about eight times a week. Now that, I can't imagine doing! I've asked him about it. Basically, he goes into character, and then he's doing the play. It's new that day. I think it has to be like that. For me, for example, with playing the *Goldberg Variations* the challenge is that it is very tiring, indeed, very exhausting, to play. It takes about 90 minutes during which I'm not leaving the stage. I need to be super focused and have an incredible amount of energy. Sometimes I look ahead to performing it, and I think, "I don't know whether I can do that!"

What do you do beforehand to try to conjure this energy?
For me it is very important that I am not doing too many other things before I play it. I have to clear my head so that I don't have other music jingling around in my head or other thoughts. The main thing is that it is hard for me to keep my mind from wandering during a performance.

Has it ever wandered?
Oh, yes [*laughs*].

Has an audience ever shown rude behavior you had to address?
The thing that I find the most difficult is when people sit in the front row and beat along with the music. Inevitably they're not beating on time, or they're a little bit restless. It's very hard for me because they're right there. I've even thought that when I'm a little further along in my career, for every concert that I play I'll just buy those tickets for the front row, so that nobody sits there. I remember one time I was playing the Emperor Concerto. Because the stage was very small, the piano was all the way on the edge of the stage, and right next to me was a man wearing an acid-green shirt. He was fidgeting around, and because he was in this extremely bright-green shirt, I just saw this green thing moving around in my line of vision. One thing that is helpful to me is that I'm used to my son running in and out of the room while I'm practicing, and I just play without thinking about that. I do think I have pretty good focus in general. Sometimes people say to me afterward, "Did you hear such and such?" And I didn't hear it at all, as I was so focused. But there is something about the visual thing that I find the most troubling, much more than the sound.

Tell me about the audience at Le Poisson Rouge in the Village where you've played a number of times. It's a totally different venue.

I think the audience there is probably the same audience that hears my other performances. It's just much more relaxed. People are eating and drinking there, so I don't worry about the movement there. It is a wonderful place, and a great idea to be mixing genres. The past couple of times I've played there, I played just by myself. The first time I played, however, the program started with an indie rock group which I followed in the same concert. I like that very much because it's interesting to combine two different genres in one performance so that people are coming to hear both kinds of music.

How particular are you about the instruments that you play?

I'm really particular. I can't sound like myself if I'm playing on a piano that's not set up right, because my playing is very light. I need a piano that is very responsive because I'm not into pushing the sound. I'm into drawing the sound out and so it needs to respond quickly. So a piano has to be set up for that. It's very important to have a really great piano technician to work on the instrument with me before the concert and get it to where I like it. I don't always know in advance of a concert who the technician is, but I usually spend quite a few hours working with the technician. In cases where they allow it, I bring along my own technician.

What instrument do you work on at home?

At the moment, a friend of mine is lending me her Steinway, so I don't feel that I can really make adjustments to her instrument. In a few years I hope to have my own instrument. I want to get a Hamburg Steinway D.

Oh, great . . . all the way! What about the space?

Well, I think the money is more important than the space actually! We had an issue when we brought in the first piano, my Baldwin. It didn't get around the hall into my room, so we had to knock a hole in the wall between the rooms to get the piano in. I was perfectly happy to knock the whole wall out!

Tell me your thoughts about the Fazioli. I know you've had experience with the instrument on tour.

I think that the Fazioli piano is really an amazing instrument. They have a lot of power and they're very, very light. It's like driving a sports car. Any movement that you make is instantly responsive. So they're the ideal concerto piano because they will really project through a huge orchestra in a big hall. So for that tour, I traveled with that piano to quite a few venues. This was the large model, just under their largest 10-foot model. In thinking about the Steinway and the Fazioli, they are completely different kinds of pianos. People are very used to the sound of the Steinway piano and often don't know how to accept the sound of the Fazioli because it has a different quality that is laser clear.

What do you think of the Hamburg Steinway?
I generally prefer them, but there's always an exception to the rule. For my recording of the *Goldberg Variations* and the Beethoven cello sonatas I used my favorite piano, a Hamburg D from the turn of the century. This 1903 instrument has a much more lyrical sound which is very different from the Steinways today. For the Berlin Concert CD I used a Hamburg instrument which I really liked, but it took about eight hours adjusting that piano to make it right for the recording.

What music do you think you will play in the future? Any Chopin, for example?
Chopin maybe, but I really like Schubert a lot, and want to play more of his music. Then, of course, Schumann and Brahms. I'm curious to learn more French music because I've hardly done any solo music; I've done a lot more chamber music. I'm thinking Debussy more than Ravel. Of course, Beethoven is one of my favorites. If I could record all of the concertos, I would love to do that!

How do you find the time and mental space to learn new music?
It's difficult. I now have a month when I get home and I will work during that time. It's really hard to figure it all out, because when I'm not performing I also want to be with my family. But I have discovered that I learn much more quickly than I thought I did. I used to spend such a long time working on the same piece. Actually I've found out that I can learn something in one or two weeks and get it to a pretty high standard. But for me personally, I like to have a lot of experience performing the same music because it develops and I feel more comfortable. So I need to learn things far in advance so that I have time for the music to jell.

Do you play for friends whose ears you trust?
Yes, I do a lot of house concerts. But I'm not looking for feedback from my friends. I'm not really focused on their response, but rather on the fact that my performance changes when there are other people in the room. I try to do a lot of playing things through. For instance, this past summer I played the Liszt Second Concerto with the New York Philharmonic. I had to learn it

in two months, which was incredibly challenging for me to learn something that quickly, and a piece of music that I would never have thought to play. In the end I really enjoyed playing it, but it was not a work that I would have picked myself. That kind of situation is really very different from how I like to do things. To learn it that fast and play it so soon.

Is there piano literature that the public doesn't hear very often but that you feel should be heard more frequently?
Oh, yes, I feel strongly that contemporary music should be heard more often. For instance, I feel very committed to Philip's *Twelve Variations*.[10] Because of my recording and performing it frequently, he's sold loads of copies of the score. I'm really proud of that, because now a lot of people have an awareness of his music. He's actually writing a piano concerto for me right now. I'm always on the lookout for music that I really relate to. Composers send me music all the time. I think one of the problems for composers is that they often get a premiere, and then their music is never played again. So I try to look for music that is going to have longevity and that I want to play more than once.

Are there other composers you may want to explore?
I like Dutilleux whose chamber music I know, but not his solo piano music. Sofia Gubaidulina is interesting to me. And I do like some Kurtág that I've heard. I've not played any of his pieces myself, only listened to them. I should mention that I really like George Crumb and his music. There are a few composers I've commissioned, for example, Jefferson Friedman. Nico Muhly is writing a solo piece of about 15 minutes for me. I'm actually doing a very interesting project in 2011 with Tift Merritt[11] who is a folk singer and songwriter. I really like her. We're commissioning composers to write for us, including Brad Mehldau, the jazz pianist.[12] I'm really looking forward to playing with Tift, because again I feel strongly that there is a dialogue to be had between different genres, and I want to promote that.

Changing the subject completely. How do you handle the daily stress of the traveling you do? Do you do yoga, for instance?
I should be doing it, but this past year everything has rather gone to pits in terms of exercise. I was doing yoga in my room for a long time—which is very good to do. You know, it's hard and challenging because it's unnatural to travel this much. I'm starting to do things like carry my own food with me. We've just bought a little computer so that I'm going to try doing Skype with my son because he is not good on the phone. I'm hoping that seeing each other might be easier for everyone. While I'm at home I try to do all my work

while he's in school or while he's asleep, so that the hours that he is at home I'm with him. That's important. Also, I try to go into his classroom and help out, so that he sees me there, too.

You've started a musical series in his school, the PS 321 Neighborhood Classics there in Brooklyn. You engage artists to donate their performances to raise funds for the school. That's gone well?
Yes, it's great. I didn't play for the first concert, but my brother-in-law played, and raised $4,000 for the school.

Are there others who are joining you by going into other public schools?
Along this line, I'm seriously thinking of starting a nonprofit in New York that would help this to happen in many schools. It's a lot of work that I've not had the time to get to yet.

You've worked frequently with your friend, the fine cellist Zuill Bailey, who is on the faculty at the University of Texas at El Paso. Are there other artists you would really enjoy a chance to collaborate with? What about a singer?
It's my dream to play with Renée Fleming! Isn't she wonderful? I also like Dawn Upshaw. As for violinists, I would absolutely love to play with Christian Tetzlaff, if I could ever meet him, and also with Gidon Kremer. This year I'm playing with the Chiara String Quartet, which is a young quartet and one of my favorites. We've played a lot together. I'm getting together with Richard Stoltzman, the clarinetist, who is coming over to my home soon to play with me. It may be that we will do something together. Perhaps Brahms and Schumann. And we're talking about doing one of the Bach gamba sonatas, which would be interesting!

Thanks so very much for your generous time in sharing your insights.

Select Discography

Bach: A Strange Beauty. With Kammerorchester Staatskapelle Berlin. "Ich ruf zu Dir, Jesu Christ," arr. Busoni; Keyboard Concerto # 5 in F Minor; "Nun freut euch, lieben Christen g'mein," arr. Kempff; English Suite # 3 in G Minor; Keyboard Concerto # 1 in D Minor; "Jesu, Joy of Man's Desiring," arr. Hess. Recorded June 2010. Sony Classical 88697 81742 2. Liner notes by Simone Dinnerstein, and an interview with Alan Rusbridger. 2011.

Ludwig van Beethoven. *Complete Works for Piano and Cello*. Zuill Bailey, cello, and Simone Dinnerstein, piano. Telarc International 2CD-80740. 2009.

The Berlin Concert. J. S. Bach. French Suite in G major. Philip Lasser. *Twelve Variations on a Chorale by J. S. Bach* ("Nimm von uns, Herr, du treuer Gott" from Cantata 101). Ludwig van Beethoven. Sonata in C Minor, op. 111. Encore: Bach. Variation 13 from *Goldberg Variations*. Recorded live 22 Nov. 2007 at the Berlin Philharmonie. Telarc International CD-80715. 2008.

J. S. Bach. *Goldberg Variations*. Telarc International CD-80692. Liner notes by Simone Dinnerstein. 2007. Won Diapason d'Or Award in 2008.

Notes

1. Maria Curcio. Five of Curcio's pianists remembered her after her death in 2009. Chloe Cutts's "Music Beyond Words," *International Piano* 5 (Sept./Oct. 2009), 32–35.

2. Solomon Mikowsky (b. 1936) at the Manhattan School of Music in New York City.

3. Peter Serkin (b. 1947), son of pianist Rudolf Serkin, at the Juilliard School of Music. Serkin is known for playing Schubert and Beethoven, and as a founding member of the group Tashi.

4. Barry Douglas (b. 1960), Irish pianist who won the 1986 Tchaikovsky Competition, and José Feghali (b. 1961), Brazilian pianist who won the 1985 Van Cliburn Competition.

5. Annie Fischer (1914–1995). Hungarian pianist who played frequently in London. Her final recital of Beethoven and Schumann was at the Royal Festival Hall in June of 1992.

6. Shura Cherkassky (1909–1995). Born in Odessa.

7. Ivo Pogorelich (b. 1958). Born in Belgrade, Yugoslavia, now Serbia.

8. Myra Hess (1890–1965). English pianist.

9. Richard and John Contiguglia (b. 1937). American duo-pianists who studied with Hess in London.

10. Philip Lasser (b. 1963). On the Juilliard faculty. In addition to making his *Twelve Variations on a Chorale by J. S. Bach* from 2002 a standard part of her solo repertoire, Dinnerstein premiered Lasser's *Chacone Variations* for violin and piano, with Fenella Barton at Wigmore Hall in 2008.

11. Tift Merritt (b. 1975). See "Second Album Syndrome" in *Gramophone* from September 2008 for a conversation between Dinnerstein and Merritt.

12. Jefferson Friedman (b. 1974), Nico Muhly (b. 1981), and Brad Mehldau (b. 1970) are prominent among the rising younger generation of American composers.

Marc-André Hamelin. Photo by Louise Narboni/CLC Productions

~

CHAPTER FOUR

Marc-André Hamelin

Marc-André Hamelin was born in Montréal on the 5th of September in 1961. His father was a pharmacist by profession. As a keen amateur pianist, he interested his son quite early in music for the piano and guided his early training.

Many of the finest pianists playing at the beginning of the 21st century are wildly fiery in their performances, seductively drawing their audiences toward their flame. Hamelin stands apart from these in that he presents an uncommonly placid presence at the piano even during the heat of the battle in his most daring pianism. He gives the aura of a cool wizard, producing magical tricks of dexterity playing some of the piano's most daunting literature while outwardly showing little effort in their production. More than one critic has remarked on this aspect of Hamelin's live performances, some commenting on occasion that he makes the difficult seem ordinary and somehow not quite compelling despite his superb technical facility. On the other hand, no one has ever disputed the wide range of his musical curiosity, which has led him to perform live and to record vast swaths of the piano's most difficult, frequently unsung works, which few have dared to spend the time to learn in order to commit to record. This is his strength, and indeed what he hopes is his legacy.

If Hamelin brings Alkan, Medtner, Godowsky, and Scriabin to a wider audience and has generated in them a closer relationship to the music of these overlooked masters, then he feels that his time and effort spent over a lifetime of learning their music has been worth his labor of love. The virtuosity required to perform these composers does not interest him as much as the inherent music in their compositions. Hamelin is adamant about not playing music that holds no emotional or musical interest for him. He readily admits that he is drawn to these particular composers because their music is complex, dense, and harmonically rich.

From 1996 to 1998 Hamelin sat down with Robert Rimm for a series of extensive conversations about eight composer-pianists on whom Rimm had begun writing a book.[1] Rimm wanted to talk with Hamelin after he heard him in a series of three New York recitals in 1996. He later discovered that the two of them were neighbors in Philadelphia.

Rimm was researching and studying the personalities and lives, performance careers, and music of Charles-Valentin Alkan (1813–1888), Kaihosru Shapurji Sorabji (1892–1988), Ferruccio Busoni (1866–1924), Leopold Godowsky (1870–1938), Samuel Feinberg (1890–1962), Alexander Scriabin (1872–1915), Nikolai Medtner (1880–1951), and Sergei Rachmaninoff (1873–1943), and had begun to call them The Eight. Each of the eight was a brilliant pianist who performed his own music, and who knew each other's music well. These eight were to be among the last in a long line of pianists who expressed themselves freely in music for their instrument. Soon after World War II, pianists no longer felt this same urge to express themselves in writing for themselves. But near the end of our last century, several fine pianists, including Hamelin, are found to be returning to this art. This and the fact that Hamelin was playing The Eight[2] brought Rimm to the decision to include him in his book. Thus developed their series of conversations. Rimm devotes one chapter exclusively to Hamelin, letting him speak about his personal journey in studying and playing the music of The Eight. Hamelin also reveals much about his own work as a composer. He explains how his own composition relates to what he has learned from playing the music of other composers. The magic of composition continues to fascinate him.

Lest one think that Hamelin has devoted himself as a pianist to the music of composers who belong solely to the rich harmonic tradition found at the end of the 20th century, or who are no longer living, one has only to note that when he was only 13 he managed to buy, and carefully kept out of his father's sight, John Kirkpatrick's seminal recording of Charles Ives's *Concord* Sonata and the score. This led to his youthful exploration of the music of Boulez, Cage, Stockhausen, and Xenakis. But it was certainly Ives's sonata that was groundbreaking for Hamelin's growth. He first recorded it for New World Records in 1988, and for a second time for Hyperion in 2004 to celebrate the 50th anniversary of Ives's death.

As for living composers, in 1987 Hamelin worked with William Bolcom, and recorded his *Twelve New Études* for New World Records. More recently Hamelin worked with the South African–Irish composer Kevin Volans (b. 1949) on his extremely difficult piano concerto *Atlantic Crossing*, giving the premiere under Michael Tilson Thomas with the San Francisco Symphony in November 2006. Volans is a fan of Hamelin's playing and wrote his concerto expressly for him. Hamelin and I spoke of several other living composers in our conversation.

Among those we spoke of is the Ukrainian-born Nicolai Kapustin (b. 1937), who attracted Hamelin's attention after becoming one of the musical surprises of the 1990s after the fall of the Soviet Union. Kapustin managed to absorb American jazz to his very core while living his isolated musical life in Moscow during the Soviet era. Under these influences, he wrote dozens of pieces for the piano in his signature highly virtuosic jazz style, but couched in traditional forms. Hamelin has championed Kapustin's complex music by recording a disc in 2003 for Hyperion devoted exclusively to Kapustin's music.[3] Earlier, Hamelin was pleased to have been able to perform his Second Sonata during a series of concerts at the Blackheath Music Halls in Southeast London in May of 2000, with the composer present.

We should not lose sight of the fact that Hamelin has never lost interest in playing the standard solo repertoire. Allan Kozinn said it best when he commented on Hamelin's "omnivorous approach to the keyboard repertory" and "his interpretive imagination" that "is so flexible that he seems completely at home in just about everything he touches."[4] In 2007 and 2008 Hamelin featured Beethoven's last three piano sonatas, and Chopin's Second and Third Sonatas frequently on his recitals. In 2009 Hyperion released his Chopin recording featuring the Second and Third Sonatas, and later his recording of Beethoven's last three sonatas.

Hamelin is quite modest in speaking about his own compositional efforts, admitting that his basic language is tonal, with much chromaticism thrown in. In 2010 Peters Edition published his *12 Études in All the Minor Keys*, the first printing of which quickly sold out. The final piece of the set is a Prelude and Fugue in A-flat Minor dating from 1986.[5] It is the earliest piece here that he composed. The difficult four-part fugue occupied him for nine months, and only after its completion did he realize that he had been influenced by the fugue of Samuel Barber's Piano Sonata. He also discovered he had absorbed much from Sergei Taneyev's Prelude and Fugue, op. 29, and from the fourth movement of Busoni's Piano Concerto.[6] The set's last piece was composed in 2007. Hamelin recorded the *Études* for Hyperion, and played a program of them at Le Poisson Rouge in September of 2010.

His *Con intimissimo sentimento* is a cycle of seven pieces for the piano he brought together from sketches, again made over a few years. It is generally not as difficult as some of his music,[7] for example, his transcription of Zequinha de Abreu's *Tico-Tico no Fubá*,[8] which incidentally the Italian pianist Sandro Russo plays.

Hamelin came to international attention when he took first prize in Carnegie Hall's International Competition of American Music in 1985, and has since played with the major orchestras around the globe, working with the most noted conductors. He has been a regular guest artist at numerous international festivals, including the Rarities of Piano Music festival at Schloss vor Husum in northern Germany, the Ravinia Festival in Chicago, and La Roque d'Anthéron in France. Louise Narboni's film *Des pas sur la neige*, made for CLC Productions in February of 2009 but unfortunately not available commercially, features Hamelin in rehearsal and in recital at Les Sommets musicaux in Gstaad. He is a frequent guest at London's Wigmore Hall.

Among his numerous honors are being made an Officer of the Order of Canada, and a Chevalier de l'ordre national du Québec, both in 2005. It is, however, for his industry as a prodigious recording artist that he has received his most notable honors. Some feel that his Hyperion recordings, begun in the mid-1990s, are largely responsible for catapulting him into the public's attention. In 2006 in Berlin, he received the recording industry's Preis der Deutsche Schallplattenkritik as acknowledgement for his complete body of recorded works. He received *Gramophone*'s Instrumental Award for 2000 for his Hyperion recording of the Godowsky Studies on Chopin Études, and was nominated in 2005 for *Gramophone*'s Artist of the Year for both his recording of Albeniz's *Iberia* and Ives's *Concord* Sonata. His performances at Schloss vor Husum have been recorded live since his first appearance there in 1989 and now number nine discs on Danacord. He is one among several artists that appear on each Danacord disc. Prior to joining Hyperion, he had also recorded for Altarus the music of Sorabji and Sophie-Carmen Eckhardt-Gramatté (1899–1974).

Frazer Jarvis, in the Department of Pure Mathematics at the University of Sheffield and himself a "keen pianist," maintains an excellent website devoted to Hamelin's recorded legacy which can be found at www.afjarvis .staff.shef.ac.uk/mah.

I spoke by phone with Hamelin midday on the 23rd of March in 2006 at his home in Philadelphia. He currently resides in the Boston area with his fiancée, Cathy Fuller.[9]

Interview

You hold a distinctive place as a pianist today because you have been wonderfully illuminating many of the mysterious corners of the piano's vast literature that have lain dormant for well over a century now. Through so many of your recordings on Hyperion, listeners now know many late 19th-century and early 20th-century composers whose works have seldom, if ever, been performed in decades.

It's a very nice position to be in. It's a little bit like antique shopping. I often compare it to that. Imagine yourself in a little town with lots of nice little antique shops, a lot that are quite dusty. They're full of quite marvelous stuff and everything on the shelf is free so you can take what you want. You can take it home, polish it up, and see how presentable you can make it.

You grew up in Montréal. Was your father your first teacher?

Well, not officially, no, but he did supervise and oversee a lot of what I was doing. I had a private teacher for four years who was moderately good, but after that, my father thought that I really needed something better, especially at the rate I was progressing. So he enrolled me in the Vincent d'Indy School when I was nine. I started at five with this private teacher.

Your father was an amateur pianist.

A very good one.

Did you play duets with him early on?

I sure did. Actually, he got me to play duets with him at the first opportunity almost, as soon as I was good enough.

Do you remember some of the things you played in those very early years?

It was everything from Wagner's *Rienzi* Overture to Leroy Anderson's *Sleigh Ride*. I remember things like the Schubert *Rosamunde* Overture.

He had quite an extensive knowledge! And he had quite an extensive library of recorded music.

Yes, and also a good amount of scores. He really had what could be termed most of the basic repertoire. I became familiar with it very early because of that, and because of the fact that I was always curious. As soon as I had a little pocket money, which was in my early teens, I started to buy some scores and records for myself, as much as my pocket money would allow.

Did this interest extend, as well, to opera and chamber music?
Everything except opera, actually. I had an education in opera at school. We analyzed quite a few of the most important ones. But I have to say that that's not where my heart really lay.

Things with text and words didn't interest you?
Things with gratuitous vocal virtuosity.

Piano virtuosity, but not vocal virtuosity!
Piano virtuosity, I think, is another animal. But, of course, that is debatable. Piano virtuosity is much more accepted as long as there is some music behind it. If there isn't, of course, I'm not interested.

Do you have your father's collection now?
Yes. Some of it is still in Canada, but I have brought a lot of it back here.

Godowsky occupied you very early, didn't he?
Yes. My father was interested in seeing Godowsky's printed music in general, but the arrangements of the Chopin études, in particular, because he had read about Godowsky's music in Harold Schonberg's book *The Great Pianists*.[10] It took awhile before he found any significant amount of the music. He did make a trip to New York in 1970 which resulted in his finding a lot of stuff, secondhand, of course. He added to his collection over the years, and I helped him a lot because of my travels. His goal was to collect all of Godowsky's sheet music. He was well on the way to doing that by the time he died in 1995.

Your father had that passion for collecting, making things "whole."
About Godowsky, I have to tell you that he was a member of the International Piano Library, which has since become the International Piano Archives at the University of Maryland. Back then, it was called the International Piano Library or IPL. The original publisher of the Chopin/Godowsky études reprinted them in 1968 or 1969 and IPL acquired a number of the sets and made them available to members. So my father was one of the first in line to get one. This means that I literally was seven years old when I saw these for the first time. I remember the day that they arrived in the mail. My dad and I sat on the edge of the bed, just looking at those bug-eyed! Neither of us had ever seen anything like it. So that was my first exposure, although limited. My father, of course, tried his hand at them trying to learn the easier ones and reading them rather extensively.

Do you perform Godowsky's *Passacaglia* live very often?
I've only played it seven or eight times, I think, ever. It's not because I don't like it. It's just because there are so many other things. There are a number of young pianists who have undertaken it. It has a daunting reputation because of some stupid remark that Horowitz made to the effect that it takes six hands to play it. Any young, hot-shot pianist who can play Rachmaninoff's Second Sonata can play the Godowsky *Passacaglia*, although I think it requires a little more intellectual probing than Rachmaninoff does. But still, it really doesn't deserve the reputation that it has.

At age nine you were in a local competition, the Canadian Music Competition.
It's still in existence. You compete in your own age group, and there are several different ones, from ages 7 to 25, I think.

Do you remember what you played at age nine?
It was a clutch of five pieces, but the most important one was the Kabalevsky *Variations*, op. 40, no. 1. The theme is just eight bars long, based on a downward D major scale. That's all it is. It's very well written for children.

You were already with Yvonne Hubert at that time, right?
No, I started when I was 11. I was with her until the time I was 18.

So you were still under your first teacher when you entered that competition?
No. At Vincent d'Indy we had nuns who were the piano teachers.

So you were with Yvonne Hubert a couple of years later?
Yes. If you've read about me you know that she had been Alfred Cortot's assistant when she was still in France.

How did you happen to go to her in particular?
Well, she had an affiliation with the Vincent d'Indy School in as much as the nuns acted as a *repétitrice* for her, in a preparatory capacity. It became imperative that I would go to her. So they prepared me for her, at the beginning monthly, then every two weeks after a while.

What literature were you studying under her at age 11 and 12?
That's going way back! I remember at age 11, two years after the big competition, my big piece was the prelude from Debussy's suite *Pour le piano*.

That was a huge step forward. Then the next year it was the *Jardins sous la pluie*. I think the year after that it was the Chopin *Andante spianato et grande polonaise*, which was really pretty big.

At about the age of 12, 13, or 14, do you remember how much time you were actually spending at the piano?
I never spent a great deal of time, I think. You have to realize that I really did have a natural facility. A good capacity for learning. Memorization has never been a problem. It's not as easy now that I'm 44 because I don't absorb as well, nor retain as well.

You were a very quick learner.
Yes, because I'm very analytical. I try to approach and retain a piece from every possible angle—form, harmony, rhythm, melody, or whatever.

Then Harvey Wedeen came to the Vincent d'Indy School.
Yes. It was all due to a colleague of mine, a celebrated teacher in the Montréal area, Marc Durand. He had gone to Temple University and ended up studying with Harvey Wedeen. After Yvonne Hubert's retirement, when the school was looking for a master teacher, Marc suggested Harvey Wedeen. So Harvey Wedeen made the trip for a few years to Montréal every month. That's where we met. Then he invited me to Temple University with the quasi promise of a full tuition scholarship, which is what ended up happening.

Before you went to Philadelphia, what pianists were you hearing in live performance up to about that time?
Well, I can tell you a few that I remember. In 1976 I heard Rubinstein's last recital in Montréal. I heard people like Ciccolini, Jean-Philippe Collard, de Larrocha. I used to go to the symphony concerts a lot because we could get cheap tickets, three bucks twenty-five at the very top. But at least we were there. I remember the very first recital I took myself to; I went alone. It was in 1974. It was the duo-pianist brothers Alfons and Aloys Kontarsky, who are famous for contemporary music, but at that time in Montréal they were playing a mixed program. I had known and really admired their recordings. They're not playing together anymore because one of them has had several strokes. But they're the types who can play either the Brahms two-piano sonata or the Boulez *Structures* by memory. They were really an extraordinary phenomenon.

What year did you arrive in Philadelphia?
August, 1980, and I've been here ever since.

Tell me about Wedeen's teaching. What was he teaching?
His predilection was for Baroque, Classic, and Romantic. Contemporary music was not his area of concentration, although he did go to Bartók and Prokofiev. But not any recent music.

Did he present frequent recitals so that his students could hear him play?
No, no. I only heard him play short excerpts in master classes or things like that or when he demonstrated. I have to say that I wish I had heard him more because he really had a marvelous touch especially in the "piano" range. His "piano" to "pianissimo" range was really quite exquisite. Just hearing him play the opening measures of the Chopin F Minor Nocturne, op. 55, no. 1, for example, was wonderful.

When did you meet Russell Sherman?
Well, I know that he heard me because he was one of the judges at the Carnegie Hall Competition on American Music in 1985. I went to him in 1986 and saw him semi-sporadically for a couple of years. I say sporadically because I actually had to travel to Boston.

What aspects of his teaching were important?
Well, he gave you tremendous inspiration just by what he was saying, especially by providing stimulating images, for trying to get you out of your skin. That's really what I value most. I was playing the Classical and Romantic literature with him.

Did you work on Beethoven with him?
No. I'm not sure I was that interested at the time. I'm much more interested now. Oh, I did bring at least one Beethoven sonata because the only interpretive advice I remember him giving me came when I brought him Beethoven's Sonata, op. 10, no. 2 in F Major. The passage in question was the beginning of the second half of the Trio in the second movement; brooding chords followed by a *sforzando* note in the treble and a short scale. For some reason I couldn't get the spirit quite right, and then he said: "Imagine these huge, colossal Roman temples, with these monolithic columns, and behind one of them, Julius Caesar is being murdered." Now how many teachers will go as far as this to get interpretive juice from their students?

It's marvelous! A bit exaggerated perhaps, but if that's what it takes. Just to wrap it up, all three of these teachers were extremely beneficial in their own different ways. All of them had very even tempers, which was refreshing. I realized that tenfold during my one lesson with Adele Marcus.[11] She was abusive toward just about everybody. I know that one has to be diplomatic and everything. But the kind of behavior she exhibited was extraordinarily callous. And it's a shame because she evidently had a lot to offer. Her musical education and her musical qualities were very sound. But she chose to destroy people's personality. I mean, whenever she had to tell somebody that she didn't think they were fit for a career, there are a lot more gentle ways to do that than the one she adopted, which was to insult them to the core. In my one two-hour private lesson with her, she proceeded to tell me that I wasn't an interesting musician, I didn't know how to read a score, I had no rhythm, and I couldn't count. I'll always admit to faults, but these remarks brushed aside—no, slapped in the face—20 years of work. That, I find abysmal. She said the kinds of things that can scar you psychologically for life. She really drilled to find the insecurities, and she seemed to find pleasure in that. She liked to destroy and then rebuild, but most people who were destroyed didn't hang around, and they stayed scarred. I mean, it's difficult to talk about it because over the years I've gotten angrier about it. My wife still remembers the call that I made to her from New York after the lesson and how absolutely deflated I sounded. Because I took these remarks to heart, I wasn't thinking privately, "You're full of it. You just don't know what you're saying. You're doing this artificially because I don't really deserve this." I took these matters to heart because I was still a good little boy.

My next question comes rather strangely on the heels of that. When did you realize that you were going to be a pianist?
I think it came about rather gradually, but by my early teens I think I was pretty sure. It was the only thing I felt I was really qualified for, that I showed any aptitude in. There could have been other things, but I didn't pursue them.

Over the years now, you've been exploring the music of Alkan, Medtner, Feinberg, Busoni, and of course Godowsky. I don't want to repeat a lot of what you told so well to Robert Rimm in his very fine book. But I would like to know whether upon more reflection you've changed your opinion about any of them. Have any of these been relegated to a lower status in your mind, or have some even risen more, or is it about the same?
The one figure among all of these who I've developed a very qualified admiration for over the years is Sorabji. I don't know how familiar you are with

his music. He spent most of his life writing very complex piano music and many of his pieces last quite a long time, even a few hours.

Has Sorabji risen in your estimation?
No, not really. Lowered somewhat. I still admire him. But I've come to re-alize—and I don't want to influence other pianists because if they want to learn the music and spend time with it they are more than welcome to it—that Sorabji's music really addresses a microscopic audience. I was already having doubts, but what opened my eyes even further, was that in June 2004 the New York premiere of the *Opus clavicembalisticum* (1929–1930), which is his most notorious piece for piano, took place, played by a British pianist named Jonathan Powell. Here's the New York premiere of a piece that many people wonder about and would love to hear. Guess how many people were in the audience? It was anywhere from about 60 to 75. Not good really for something for which you're going to spend 10 to 20 years of your life. If that few people come in a city like New York—which is probably the second most important musical city in the world after London—what's this? Life is short. I'm going to spend time with things that give me a little more satisfaction and better satisfaction with an audience.

Medtner's work holds a very special place for you. He's not simply a poor man's Rachmaninoff!
Oh, my gosh, no. The trouble with Medtner is that he falls apart if he's not played with absolute conviction. If you're going through the motions with him, it's just not enough. You have to highlight everything, you have to point out the form, give harmonies the time they deserve. You really have to treat him lovingly and then he'll reveal himself to you. But the problem is that with most performances he will not generally reveal himself to the listener at the first hearing. He really demands and repays repeated hear-ings.

As does most of the very best music. You've been playing long enough now around the globe to be able to make some judgments about audiences. Is there a noticeable difference in audiences?
I don't find fundamental listening differences from one country to the next. It's really from one city or one venue to another. I've really tried, but I find it impossible to generalize over the years. New York, for example, has a reputa-tion for having noisy audiences, but I've found that in many cases to be the complete opposite. A friend of mine came from the U.K. to attend a concert in Carnegie Hall and he was absolutely appalled at the level of noise from

the audience. But it's been my experience with many of the concerts I've given that the audiences were very respectful. So I really find it impossible to generalize.

What about strange and bizarre happenings at performances and how you handle some of them? I'm also thinking about bad behavior on the part of an audience.
There are cell phones, of course!

I remember reading about one of your encores recently in Houston.
Oh, yes. Well, Nokia instituted this cell phone ring [whistles the ring]. You've heard it many times, I'm sure. At one time it was almost the only one you ever heard. It's the one that Nokia phones always default to. I decided to write a little one-page waltz[12] on that theme, which, incidentally, people may not know is a little phrase—a four-bar phrase from a guitar piece by Tárrega.[13] If you look on the Net, there is a Tárrega home page that refers you to a list of MP3s. Listen to the piece. It's called *Grand valse*. I wrote this little waltz to pinpoint this person in the audience, to let him or her know that I heard. Although you do have to handle this in other ways sometimes. I played in Warsaw in early February. I played the last three Beethoven sonatas at the hall of the Warsaw Philharmonic and it was being recorded for later broadcast by the radio. A minute and a half into the first movement of opus 109 I heard, very loudly and sharply [whistles opening of the march from Tchaikovsky's *Nutcracker*]. I finished the first movement, which is about two and a half minutes long, and spoke a few words to the audience. I said I was starting again; I did this because of the radio. You remember in the 1980s, it was the beeper watches and we thought *that* was a problem [*laughs*]!

What about the high-pitched hearing aids?
Yes, that has happened a couple of times. There was one incident in Tokyo, not a hearing aid, but it was about coughing, actually. It was a Tokyo recital and I started my recital with the three *Intermezzi*, op. 117, of Brahms and as you know they are three very quiet pieces. In the middle of the first one this woman starts coughing really rather badly. She was near the front. People told me this later, because she wasn't in my line of sight. People around her were going "shh." Her husband kept telling her she should go out. But she kept saying, "No, no, I want—cough, cough—to stay here." She just wouldn't stop. Pretty soon other people started telling her she should leave. Suddenly she started justifying herself in normal voice. And I was still playing these very, very soft things. This lasted basically through the whole

thing. These pieces are about 15 minutes long. She was so recalcitrant that when I went off stage before playing the next thing, which was going to be the Schumann *Fantasy*, op. 17, I had to wait about six or seven minutes before I went back on stage. It took them that long to persuade that woman to walk off.

Television has something to do with that. People don't realize that the person who is delivering what they've come to hear is aware of them. Let's talk about recording.
I love it.

As much as live performance?
It's an arduous process, of course, to repeat things and get them as well as one can. It's an awesome feeling when—I don't mean awesome in the teenager's sense—but it's really quite a wonderful feeling when one is done. Especially when one listens to the finished product. In my case, I can say personally, that because I've done a lot of the out-of-the-way repertoire, I feel good in making a potential contribution to the appreciation to these composers. The reactions to my recordings have proven to me that in many cases this has paid off really handsomely and as much as I had hoped. There is a definite around-the-world level of interest, and it has risen.

Do you think that this has influenced other pianists?
I know that it has, especially younger ones. Many young pianists come to me after recitals asking me to autograph their scores of Medtner and Alkan, and Godowsky and things like that. Even some of my own music, too.

Which recordings of yours are you especially proud of?
There are certainly a few. Believe it or not, one of the ones I'm proudest of is the Max Reger one, because of the way it came out. By that, I assume that you mean the ones that really came closest to my intentions. Yes, the Reger is certainly one of them. The Shostokovich concerti are very valuable to me. Also the recording of the music of Nicolai Kapustin. And the Chopin/Godowsky studies, of course. There might be others but these are the ones that come to my mind at the moment. I have 30 with Hyperion already at the moment and there are four more recorded.

Hyperion's sound quality is superb. Have you given much thought about what the concept of recording has done to an audience's expectation about what they are going to hear in a live performance?

I think they want to hear the recording with the visual elements superimposed. It can be quite a challenge when you've spent a lot of time in the studio correcting mistakes. Then suddenly you're on the stage and you have just one go-around to provide a close enough facsimile of what they heard on the recording, without any mistakes whatsoever, hopefully. So that's the daunting task! I've resigned myself to the fact that it can't happen exactly. One does the best one can, of course.

Don't you wish the audience could understand the difference?
Yes. I'm told time and time again that my live performances are consistently better than my recordings, more free, for example. I don't necessarily feel that way, but if that's what they feel.

Do you feel that the audience is helping you in the performance?
When you feel they're with you, yes, and that's usually the case.

You don't have that in the studio.
Well, no. But you really have to use your imagination. I usually feel that the audience is with me. You were asking me about different countries. Places like Italy are actually very sober as far as applause. The applause is not prolonged at all. But I learned later that this is no indication of their appreciation. In contrast to that, I have to recount a wonderful occasion. I played a recital in Alice Tully Hall in 2000 and I hadn't played in New York for four years. I remember very clearly that I got to the piano and they were applauding. I bowed and then I sat down. They were applauding so much I had to get up and bow again. Can you imagine how much of a lift that gives you? It's marvelous. They're saying, "We haven't heard you in a while, and it's good that you're here." It was extraordinary.

Tell me, what do you do to handle all the stresses of travel?
I put myself in neutral psychologically as much as possible. Otherwise it would be . . . [laughs].

Do you practice yoga at all, or swim?
No, no, not really. I don't even try to keep much in shape, although I've gotten back to the gym semiregularly recently. Actually that's what I'm going to do when I finish talking with you. At least, treadmilling keeps your heart in shape. I also do some muscle-building and arm exercises.

Do you have any rituals you go through before a performance?
No. I'm very loose about that. I can even be talking with somebody before I go on stage [*laughs*].

So that's never been an issue from your youth on?
No. I don't need to be alone, concentrated, and meditating or anything like that.

I want to go back to the literature that you play. I read that you inherited a sheet-music collection from someone in Montréal who had been a disciple of Scriabin.
Actually, I inherited it from his widow because he died in 1952 and she died in 2002 [*laughs*]. She was one of his students and was very young when they got married. This is Alfred LaLiberté,[14] friend of Medtner and Scriabin; he was a remarkable pianist, teacher, and composer. He was a very astute sheet-music collector and a lot of things in this collection were things that I had never even known existed. His widow, Madeleine, looked me up after she read a magazine article about me in which I mentioned my love of Medtner and Godowsky, and since there were very few of us at the time, she wanted to find out more about me. She had a hunch that I would find many interesting things in her late husband's sheet-music collection.

Such as?
Oh, if I named composers it wouldn't help! Trust me.

Is this where Catoire[15] comes from?
Yes, this was really precious. A large part of the collection consists of Bach transcriptions, and also sonatas and sets of variations. He was very strong on these, and also on very much lesser known Russian composers, besides Medtner and Scriabin, of course. Transcriptions of works by composers other than Bach didn't seem to interest him, however.

Have you pretty much mined the depths of that collection, or are there still things you are studying?
Well, there are things that are not terribly good, but there are others that certainly are, too. Actually I've just recorded something that was part of that collection. It's not only by a composer nobody knows, but it's the only thing he ever wrote. This is the French composer Abel Decaux.[16] It's a suite of four pieces called *Clairs de lune*. They're very remarkable because they're clearly

impressionistic and atonal, but *before* Debussy and Schoenberg. They were written between 1900 and 1907, and they were published in 1913, although I don't think they're available now. They're absolutely fascinating pieces, and I used LaLiberté's own score when I recorded them as a filler to my disc of the sonata of Paul Dukas, the composer of *The Sorcerer's Apprentice*. The Decaux was written around the same period. That and other factors make the coupling very interesting. That's coming out in May. Incidentally, it's a shame that some of these wonderful scores are still unavailable, or only obtainable with great difficulty. A number of enterprises, most notably Masters Music (operated by Kalmus) and of course Dover have done wonderful things over the years, but their wish to do more has been crippled—the word is not too strong—by the present U.S. copyright laws, which state that anything created after January 1st, 1923, will forever remain in copyright. To reprint anything composed since would prove too onerous for a publisher like Dover, who only reprint copyright-free material, and who would not have the financial resources to pay copyright fees.

How can pianists today obtain the scores by Catoire and Decaux, to name just two composers?
Some years ago, Robert Rimm, who really took to Catoire's music and has a deep love for Russian culture, very enterprisingly made a volume of the complete piano music of Catoire available through his website, but this has now run out and I don't think it will be reprinted. Decaux's *Clairs de lune* could certainly be reprinted, since they're in the public domain. I hope Kalmus is listening!

Have you had a chance to play Beethoven's *Diabelli Variations* in concert?
Not yet. I haven't really learned them, although I know them very well. I used to listen to Julius Katchen's recording. It's always been a favorite of mine.

What would you program that with?
Hmm. Something like this opens up a very interesting field of possibilities. I'm not sure a hasty reply would be worthy of this kind of discussion. It's certainly interesting to consider.

Wasn't it Ursula Oppens who asked Rzewski for *The People United Will Never Be Defeated!*, his set of variations to go with the *Diabelli*?
You're right.

Is there anyone who presents one recital featuring both pieces?
It's certainly not an impossibility, although we're kind of in a minority playing the Rzewski *Variations*. Not a lot of people play these.

I must say I love that set, and I really like your recording of it.
Thank you. It is one of my favorites.

Once one hears that, it's in the mind for the day.
Especially that theme [*laughs*]! It's the kind of thing you feel like you've heard
before somewhere.

You've recorded Leo Ornstein's music. Did you ever meet Ornstein?
No, unfortunately, but I know his son very well. He lives in Woodside, Cali-
fornia. He was one of the early developers of the Internet. He's now in his
mid-70s and still fit as a fiddle. I mean, they have really incredible genes in
that family. He still climbs mountains.

**Ornstein is such a fascinating figure that it's amazing that he's not known
better.**
Yes, his works are unbelievably pianistic. If you read anything at the keyboard you realize that very quickly.

Does minimalism hold any interest for you at all?
Only when it's very well done, when it has a spirit—the right kind of spirit
behind it. I can't stand Philip Glass. I'm sorry. I once played John Adams's
Hallelujah Junction for two pianos. That's kind of fun.

How about his *Phrygian Gates,* or his *China Gates*?
No, I never did. I very much enjoy Steve Reich, and always regretted that
he's never written for solo piano. I mean anything really extensive.

Many consider Elliott Carter our greatest living composer today.
I think it's more fun for all of us to coexist than to compete for first place
[*laughs*]!

**But surely you might consider Carter a venerable composer in any case.
Just last week the University of Minnesota and the St. Paul Chamber
Orchestra presented a whole series of seminars and presentations of his**

music. Ursula Oppens was scheduled to play his *Night Fantasies*. Has that piece ever interested you?
Well, it is very interesting, but again, there are so many things and so little time. The one piece of Carter's that I have done, actually, is his Piano Quintet. I got to perform it with the best possible people and that's the Arditti Quartet. I'm glad they were in the driver's seat because playing Carter is really quite an education. Nobody else thinks like him rhythmically.

You have said that you have not played Ligeti's music because you feel that the brain has to be divided into two parts.
I think it's because I didn't spend quite enough time to be able to crack it. I do think that his first étude in particular would be simpler if I renotated it and rebarred it. I had a very hard time dealing with bar lines that don't coincide. The bar lines are in different places.

First, that takes so much time, and secondly, more pianists are playing these now.
Oh, sure. These pieces have achieved tremendous popularity.

Do you play Messiaen's music?
I've played the *Turangalila* Symphony several times. My next engagement with it is with the Pittsburgh Symphony about a year from now.

What about his solo music?
Well, I'm well acquainted with it, but I've played very little in concert. I certainly don't dislike Messiaen, but there are so many other things that are less well served.

Again, a lot of other pianists are playing Messiaen's music, so audiences do have the chance to hear his music, whereas you are playing music that others are not.
That's quite true.

I've been asking each pianist with whom I speak about what living composer he would like to have a piece from, but, of course, in your case I almost hesitate because you yourself are a composer. But, is there someone living from whom you'd like a strong piece?
It's kind of a difficult question to answer because I really have not kept up with living composers as much as I feel I should. There are a few I know very

well. Chief among them is Bill Bolcom. He's always said he'd like to write something for me but he's just beset with commissions and doesn't have the time.

So you are on friendly terms with Bolcom. Your wives are both singers.
As a duo, my wife and I have often been compared to them, but it's not a perfect comparison by any means. Their area of expertise is American music from many periods, from the Civil War to now, whereas we have done both the American and European, and its early European cabaret songs. Not quite the same thing.

Did Bolcom complete Albeniz's *Navarra* just for you?
No, no, he did that in 1965.

What prompted him to do that?
It was probably mostly done as a stylistic exercise, but I do know he loves Albeniz's music. It's not the only completion he did, by the way. He also provided endings for the third and fourth movements of the Schubert *Reliquie*, the C Major Sonata. He also completed the Liszt *Czardas macabre*. I think he did something with the *The Begger's Opera*. I'm not sure. I could be wrong about that. He was still actually sort of a performing pianist at that time, and he included all of these completions in a recital.

You've spoken of Nicolai Kapustin already. How did you discover Kapustin?
Well, it's simple. Nicolai Petrov recorded Kapustin's Second Sonata on Olympia and someone played it for me, and my jaw dropped.

He's quite an extraordinary figure. You played his music in London about six years ago now. Do you have a continuing relationship with him at all, and follow his recent music?
We e-mail from time to time.

Is his music today substantially different from what he wrote about 10 years ago?
No, it's pretty much in the same vein, although the difference now is that many people have found out about his music and they're asking him for pieces now. There's a colleague of mine in Canada who's asked him for a concertino for two pianos and percussion, and he delivered. There's someone

else who's had a flute sonata written for him. And I think the Ahn Trio had a trio written for them. He's been doing one right after another.

You've played in Russia. Did you play any of his music there?
No, because since it was my first exposure there I wanted a program that was a little more accessible and plain. If I remember correctly, it was the Bach-Busoni *Chaconne*, and Schumann's C Major *Fantasy*, and then for the second half I did the Medtner *Sonata Idyll*, which is the last sonata he wrote, and the Alkan symphony.[17]

I wondered whether anyone in Russia is playing his music there.
Now that Kapustin is published, a lot of students are taking it up. The *Toccatina*, for example, was adopted in the Trinity College in London, in the syllabus, or the Royal College. I don't remember which. One of them has it in its syllabus.

Are there other composers who were dormant in the former Soviet Union and who we should know about?
Possibly, but I would be speaking out of ignorance. Actually there is one composer that I really like. His name is Pantcho Vladigerov.[18] He was the foremost composer in Bulgaria and really rather prolific. He had about 70 opus numbers, a lot of which are piano pieces, but he also wrote one opera, one symphony, many orchestral pieces, and some songs. He's a good composer of violin music as well. He wrote music that is basically folk inspired, very exotic and colorful, very touching as well. And also very pianistic. He died in 1978.

I see that you're playing his music this spring.
Yes, there is one thing I've been carrying in my repertoire called *Sonatina concertante*, which is a marvelous piece.

Is this being received by audiences well?
Yes, although it's not that brilliant a piece, or one where the applause is likely to be delirious. I know for a fact that it is appreciated, though. It's a refreshing thing to play.

I want to ask you about your own compositions. Have you studied formally with anyone?
Yes, but before I studied, I was already doing things on my own. I've been compelled to write almost from the very beginning. But a lot of what I was

writing at age five or six made no sense because I wasn't really acquainted properly with the science of notation.

Did you study with someone at Temple?
Yes, both Maurice Wright and Matthew Greenbaum. They actually provided more inspiration than actual technique. This was not a bad thing.

Do you think pianists who compose play differently from those who don't compose?
Hmm. If they don't, I think they should. It inevitably provides pianists with more insight because it gets them not to take for granted the piece they're playing. They appreciate more the toil that a composer has to go through in order to accomplish the miracle of translating their intangible thoughts to a system of proportional notation. To me, that really is a miracle.

You've had some things published.
Very few, but yes. Everything from a six-piano transcription of the *Maple Leaf Rag*[19] to a set of Fanfares for Three Trumpets.[20]

What are you most proud of at this point?
Well, I really haven't written a lot. My contributions are really very slight. I mean I've done mostly things in the realm of transcriptions, or arrangements actually.

Are other pianists playing some of your music?
That's starting, as a few actually are. There have been performances which I'm very happy about. A few names that come to mind are Viktoria Lakiss-ova, Sandro Russo, and Laurence Lambert-Chan.

When you're in your composing mode, do you feel free to talk about what you're working on, or do you like to keep that aspect of composing mysterious so that you don't break the spell?
I'm not looking to hide anything. I'm not sure how I can describe myself.

Some composers simply will not talk. It's not that they're hiding.
It's like explaining the painting you've just done. You know, it either touches the viewer or not. If you start explaining it, then it's like cutting open the goose that lays the golden egg.

You've expressed your feelings about not teaching. Do you think you might ever teach in the future?
Well, I do very occasionally. There is one student who I see from time to time whenever we can coordinate our schedules. But I think that if I eventually make any contribution to the realm of teaching, it will be in writing. Either writing articles, or a book. I have been accumulating notes over the years, mostly pertaining to musical rather than pianistic matters. The kind of thing that most musicians could benefit from, not only pianists.

You contributed to Dover editions of Medtner's music.
Yes, my main role in the edition of the sonatas was proofreading the whole thing. Quite a task! In the *Fairy Tales* edition I provided a little preface.[21] I was one of three people who did.

Daniel Barenboim wrote some years ago that the greatest achievement an artist can attain is that of the independence to do what he wants to do because he believes in it so strongly. What measure of independence do you feel you've achieved at this point?
I think my situation is very enviable in that respect because, for example, of Hyperion and the niche that they have and the fact that what I do really agrees with their philosophy. I think I've been doing that for years. I've been almost completely independent for years. And I don't take it lightly. I appreciate every single opportunity.

I want to thank you so much for sharing time to talk about your background, the music you're interested in and are bringing to life, both in recording and in live performances. It's been a real pleasure for me.
You're very welcome.

Select Discography

Charles Ives. *Concord* Sonata. Maurice Wright. *Sonata.* New World Records. 1992.

Hyperion

Marc-André Hamelin. *12 Études in All the Minor Keys; Little Nocturne;* five pieces from *Con intimissimo sentimento; Theme and Variations (Cathy's Variations) 2007.* CDA 67789. 2010.

Frederic Chopin. Sonata # 2 in B-flat Minor, op. 35. Sonata # 3 in B Minor, op. 58. *Berceuse* in D-flat Minor, op. 57. *Barcarolle* in F-sharp Minor, op. 60. Nocturnes op. 27, # 1 and # 2. CDA 67706. 2009.

Leopold Godowsky. *Strauss Transcriptions and Other Waltzes*. CDA 67626. 2008.

In a State of Jazz. Works by Charles Trenet, Friedrich Gulda, Nicolai Kapustin, Alexis Weissenberg, Johnny Hess and Paul Misraki, and George Antheil. CDA 67656. Liner notes by Hamelin. 2008.

Franz Joseph Haydn. Piano Sonatas. CDA 67554. Ten Sonatas on two discs, vol. 1. 2007.

Charles-Valentin Alkan. Selections from *Concerto for Solo Piano*, op. 39. *Troisième recueil de chants*. CDA 67569. 2007.

Samuel Barber. Piano Sonata. Charles Ives. *Concord* Sonata. CDA 67469. 2004.

Dmitri Shostakovich. Piano Concerto # 1, op. 35. Rodion Shchedrin. Piano Concerto # 2, "Chimes," (1967). BBC Scottish Symphony. Andrew Litton, conductor. CDA 67425. 2003.

Kaleidoscope. Works by Edna Benz Woods, Sergei Rachmaninoff, Josef Hoffmann, Felix Blumenfeld, Jacques Offenbach, Jules Massenet, Moritz Moszkowski, Francis Poulenc, Leopold Godowsky, Aleksander Michalowski, Arthur Vincent Lourié, Émile-Robert Blanchet, Alfredo Casella, John Vallier, Alexander Glazunov, Glazunov-Hamelin, Nicolai Kapustin, and Marc-André Hamelin. CDA 67275. 2001.

Leopold Godowsky. Sonata in E Minor. *Passacaglia*. CDA 67300. 2002.

Leopold Godowsky. *Études after Chopin*. CDA 67411/2. 1998–1999. Won 2000 Gramophone Instrumental Award.

The Composer-Pianists. Shorter works by Charles-Valentin Alkan, Ferruccio Busoni, Samuel Feinberg, Leopold Godowsky, Marc-André Hamelin, Nicolai Medtner, Sergei Rachmaninov, Alexander Scriabin, and Kaikhosru Sorabji. CDA 67050. 1998.

Max Reger. *Variations on a Theme by J. S. Bach*, op. 81. *Variations on a Theme by G. P. Telemann. Fünf Humoresques*, op. 20. CDA 66996. 1999. Won Gramophone Critics Choice Award.

Georgy Catoire. Selected smaller pieces. CDA 67090. 1999.

Live at Wigmore Hall. Virtuoso Romantic Series. CDA 66765. Beethoven-Alkan; Chopin-Balakirev; Alkan; Busoni; Medtner. June 1994.

On Danacord

Selections from the nine live discs *Piano Rarities at Schloss vor Husum*. Hamelin is not the sole performer on each disc.

Piano Rarities at Schloss vor Husum. Frederic Chopin/Leopold Godowsky and Zez Confrey. DACOCD 349. 1989.

Piano Rarities at Schloss vor Husum. Percy Grainger, Marc-André Hamelin, Vladimir Deshevov, and Stefan Wolpe. DACOCD 399. 1992.

Piano Rarities at Schloss vor Husum. Frederic Chopin/Franz Liszt, Salvatore Sciarrino, and Eugene Goossens. DACOCD 649. 2004.

Piano Rarities at Schloss vor Husum. Pancho Vladigerov and Charles-Valentin Alkan. DACOCD 669. 2006.

On DVD

Legato: The World of the Piano. Marc-André Hamelin: No Limits. Interview with Jan Schmidt-Garre and complete recital featuring Haydn's E Major Sonata, Chopin's B Minor Sonata, and Debussy's *Preludes*, Book II. 183 minutes. Euroarts. DVD 2055788. 2007.

It's All About the Music: The Art of Marc-André Hamelin. Shot on location in Vancouver, Philadelphia, Scotland, and Québec. Hyperion DVDA68000. 121 minutes. 2006.

Notes

1. Robert Rimm, *The Composer-Pianists: Hamelin and the Eight*, foreword by Stephen Hough (Portland, OR: Amadeus Press, 2002).

2. Hamelin has been most important in shedding light on the music of Alkan and Godowsky for our era.

3. Steven Osborne earlier recorded for Hyperion an entire disc, released in 2000, devoted to Kapustin's piano music. The selections of Hamelin and Osborne do not overlap.

4. Allan Kozinn, "Rationality Meeting Romanticism," *The New York Times*, 13 May 2011.

5. Published by Editions Doberman-Yppan of St. Nicolas, Québec, in 1993. Later with the *12 Études in All the Minor Keys* by Peters Edition in 2010.

6. Rimm, 177–178.

7. Published by Ongaku-No-Tomo-Sha in 2004.

8. Published by Schott in *The Virtuoso Piano Transcription Series*.

9. A photo of Hamelin at his piano in his Boston residence accompanies an interview with Ethan Iverson in December 2008. Interview is devoted to Hamelin's wide-ranging interest in the piano's literature. Found on Iverson's website, *Do the Math*.

10. Harold Schonberg, *The Great Pianists* (London: Gollancz, 1964).

11. Adele Marcus (1905–1995).

12. *Valse irritation après Nokia.*

13. Francisco Tárrega (1852–1909).

14. Alfred LaLiberté (1899–1952) was born in Saint-Jean d'Iberville, Québec, studied in Berlin, and taught most of his life in Montréal. Madeleine LaLiberté gave much of his legacy to the Music Archives at the National Library in Ottawa, Canada, during the mid-1990s.

15. Georgy Catoire (1861–1926). Russian composer of French heritage. Hamelin has recorded one disc, released in 1999, dedicated to his smaller works.

16. Abel Decaux (1869–1943).

17. From his *Twelve Études in the Minor Keys*, op. 39.

18. Pantcho Vladigerov (1899–1978).

19. *Maple Leaf Rag* for six pianos. Printed only by request by Theodore Presser.

20. *Fanfares.* Theodore Presser, 2003.

21. Nikolai Medtner, *Complete Fairy Tales for Solo Piano*, foreword by Hamish Milne; introduction by Marc-André Hamelin; translator's notes by Stanley Greenbaum (New York: Dover Publications, 2001). Hamelin provided editorial notes to Dover's two volumes of editions of Medtner's complete sonatas, published in 1998.

Stephen Hough. Photo by Grant Hiroshima

CHAPTER FIVE

~

Stephen Hough

Stephen Hough was born on the 22nd of November in 1961 in Heswall on the Wirral Peninsula in the north of England into a family not noted for its musical activity. When only five years old he begged for a piano and his mother saw to it that her young son had an instrument as well as a teacher. Both parents smoothed the way for his musical development. His earliest influential teacher was the 18-year-old Heather Slade-Lipkin, who was daughter of one of his mother's friends. She has since become a widely regarded teacher of pianists. After one year of instruction with her, Hough, as the youngest competitor at about age seven, placed in the finals of the National Junior Piano Playing Competition. Gerald Moore was on that jury and noted that Hough showed a lot of potential as a pianist. The publicity that ensued was a frightening experience because many concert managers came forward to thrust him into the limelight. Luckily his parents were wise enough not to push him into that arena at his age.

Slade-Lipkin soon sent her student to her own teacher, Gordon Green in Liverpool. Hough credits Green with great wisdom in having enormous care in nurturing him as a young musician with regard to long-term success as a musician, rather than exploiting him for quick celebrity. Under his care, Hough won the piano section of the BBC Young Musician of the Year Competition in 1978. On those trips to Liverpool he relished the total environment that Green offered: conversations about music, listening to recordings, and attending recitals at Philharmonic Hall. Green opened up the wider music world for Hough. After Green fell ill, Hough studied with

Derrick Wyndham at the Royal Northern College of Music in Manchester. Wyndham is also spoken of highly as Hough recalls how he taught him to practice correctly.

While Hough was obsessed with the piano until about the age of 10, his early teen years found him indulging in rock and pop music, and merely going through the motions of working at the piano. It took his composition teacher, Douglas Steele, to bring him back to serious music by playing for his student on the piano a passage of a moving chord sequence from Elgar's *The Dream of Gerontius*.[1] It was the elder British composer's music, depicting Gerontius's death with the priest praying over his body, that became a profound experience for the young Hough. Hough was to become a Catholic, as was Elgar. As well, he was inspired to buy John Barbirolli's recording of Elgar's music. With his musical fire once again lit, he returned more seriously to his study at the piano.

At age 19 Hough entered the master's degree program at Juilliard. After two years he began his doctorate, which he discontinued after he won the 1983 Naumburg International Piano Competition at age 21. He captured international attention with his New York debut recital in 1984 at Alice Tully Hall.

Hough has a high regard for scholarship devoted to the history of his instrument and its literature. He himself continues to explore the largely ignored corners of the literature, especially the music that once had major importance. He took on the project of recording Johann Nepomuk Hummel's concertos, because of the important role that Hummel's A Minor Concerto had played in the history of the development of 19th-century piano literature. Chopin, Mendelssohn, Schumann, and Liszt all played and revered Hummel's piano compositions.

By the end of this decade, Hough had recorded over 50 discs for the Hyperion label. For a number of these, he has written fine essays for the liner notes, which have been singled out by critics as being exemplary for their keen insights. For his recording of York Bowen's music, Hough describes how he discovered this gifted English pianist and composer, born in 1884, who had been praised by Saint-Saëns and Sorabji. Although Bowen fell into obscurity after he was injured in World War I, he has more recently become known as the "English Rachmaninoff." A number of Hough's liner notes appear on his website, www.stephenhough.com, along with his short essays devoted to topics that include memories of his pianist friend Joseph Villa who died all too young in 1995, Chopin and piano technique, and the demise of the German Bechstein piano. Since 2008, Hough has contributed his very frequent blog essays to his website at London's *Telegraph*.

Hough's liner notes for his 1996 Hyperion recording of the music of Catalonian Frederico Mompou (1893–1987) reveal much about his own distinctive musical ideals and pianism. For here, we discover Hough's charming childlike wonder and joy in simplicity that contributes to his love of the piano's magical sonority, found most notably in Mompou. While Hough's playing includes that of the utmost virtuosity found in the most demanding literature such as Brahms's Second and Rachmaninoff's Third Concertos, we find that he returns time again to music such as that of Mompou, where his keen ear gives him ample opportunity to capitalize on his superb ability to reveal the piano's multiple shades of color. It is not by chance that he offers Mompou frequently as an encore, for Mompou's music had a special place in his youthful development. The first recording he owned contained the *"Jeunes filles au jardin"* from his *Scènes d'enfants*. Hough has commented that he was familiar with Mompou's music prior to learning that of Bach, Beethoven, or Brahms.

Hough encourages pianists to compose for their instrument, no matter whether the composition is likely to be a masterpiece. The act of composing makes the pianist realize the core value of the piano music that others have written. As have several of the pianists playing at the beginning of the 21st century, Hough realizes that each of the greatest pianists playing at the end of the 19th and the beginning of the 20th centuries was also actively involved as a composer. Perhaps some pianists were not very great composers but nevertheless contributed to their instrument. Hough has given considerable thought to why pianists during the middle of the 20th century turned away from composing for themselves. He speaks frequently about this issue in interviews.

Hough began his creative work making transcriptions of songs that he could play as encores. Most notable are four virtuosic transcriptions of Rodgers and Hammerstein songs heard on his *New Piano Album*. With encouragement from colleagues he easily moved on to composing original compositions, beginning with pieces such as his "Musical Jewellery Box" and an "*Étude de concert*," both of which are recorded on his *New Piano Album*. His *Suite Osmanthus* is a set of six contrasting pieces, dedicated to his friend Dennis Chang. The suite is unified by two motives, one of which is based on the initials DC, and the second with Hough's own initials S (E-flat) and H (B). He recorded the suite in 2003 for *The Stephen Hough Piano Collection*. *Suite R-B* was composed in 2002, and was recorded by James Giles for a 2006 Albany Records release.[2] Later comes his sonata for piano, *Broken Branches*, which he premiered in 2011.

Hough has further moved to writing for other solo instruments, and for the orchestra, as well as for a vocal quartet. He conducted the 2007 performance of his new cello concerto in Liverpool to positive critical reviews. He has also written two mass settings: his *Mass of Innocence and Experience* for Westminster Abbey and his *Missa Mirabilis* for Westminster Cathedral. Both were premiered in London in the summer of 2007. His *Other Love Songs*, written for the vocal quartet, The Prince Consort, premiered at Wigmore Hall in June of 2011.

Hough is generous to his contemporaries by performing their music. He is known for playing the music of his two American colleagues George Tsontakis (b. 1951) and Lowell Liebermann (b. 1961). Tsontakis's demanding 30-minute *Ghost Variations* from 1991, and Liebermann's two piano concertos are both standards in Hough's repertoire. Liebermann's Second Concerto was premiered by Hough in 1992 under Rostropovich and is dedicated to Hough. He gives equal time to fellow Englishmen Stephen Reynolds (b. 1947), Alan Rawsthorne (1905–1971), and Kenneth Leighton (1929–1988).

At the piano, Hough is physically animated, revealing a dramatic, passionate temperament that places him among the fiery Dionysian performers playing today. Audiences are frequently surprised to find him approaching the piano on stage dressed completely in black, sporting red velvet or glittery turquoise shoes. He makes regular appearances at the world's major festivals including Aspen, Edinburgh, and the Proms, appearing with leading orchestras such as the Chicago Symphony Orchestra, the Philadelphia Orchestra, and the London Symphony Orchestra. As a recitalist one finds him frequently at Wigmore Hall in London and in New York's major halls.

Hough's early recording of Hummel's piano concertos with the English Chamber Orchestra brought him his first Gramophone Award. His seventh award was for his highly praised set of Rachmaninoff's concertos that was recorded live in 2004 during a three-week period under Andrew Litton with the Dallas Symphony Orchestra. Hough and his long-time friend Litton found the experience of working together on Rachmaninoff immensely satisfying.

Hough's far-reaching mind extends to more than a passing interest in writing poetry and short stories, reading philosophy, and studying theology. His *The Bible as Prayer* was published by Continuum in 2007. He contributed a personal reflection on his own life, especially as it relates to his becoming a Catholic at the age of 19, in a chapter that appeared in Ben Summerskill's book on the state of gay and lesbian artistic life in Great Britain.[3] To celebrate the 150th anniversary of the birth of fellow Englishman Sir Edward

Elgar in 2007, Hough contributed to *Elgar: An Anniversary Portrait*.[4] Early in 2008 Hough's poem "Early Rose" brought him the first prize in the Sixth International Poetry Competition.

Hough was in Chicago preparing for his performance of Beethoven's Fifth Concerto with the Grant Park Orchestra under Carlos Kalmar as part of the Grant Park Music Festival when I spoke with him by phone on the afternoon of 17 August 2006. I began by asking about the MacArthur Fellowship, since he was the first performing musician to have been granted one of the "genius" awards. The year after our conversation, in December of 2007, Hough was awarded Northwestern University's $50,000 Jean Gimbel Lane Prize in Piano Performance. He spent several stints working with students at Northwestern University throughout the 2008–2009 academic year.

Interview

Thank you so much for taking time to speak with me this afternoon and being part of my larger project. I want to begin by asking you about the MacArthur Fellowship that you received in 2001. If I understand it, this will be the last year that you will be granted part of that fellowship.
That's true. I have one more payment to come. It comes quarterly, and there is a final payment that comes in October, which will be my farewell to the MacArthur.

When you received this, what did you begin to think that this would give you the freedom to do that you couldn't do before?
It's interesting because of what they say to you. First of all, they don't care what you use the money on. You don't have to report back to them about it, or anything like that. But they presume that the people they've chosen will use it, obviously not just responsibly, but creatively as well. It's not just, for instance, for me to make more recordings, which I'm already doing anyway with my career. They suggested, for instance, that somebody might want to take six months off from working and do research. I thought of all sorts of possibilities. I thought that one thing that was holding me back a little bit was the inability to work in London in my house late at night, and at all times, because of neighbors. So what I actually decided to do with it was build myself, or create, a studio, which was soundproof where I could go and work forever without really having to hold back. This was something that would not last for just five years, but would really last for my whole career. So that's what I did. I found a flat just a couple of streets away from where I

lived. It's a basement flat with a garden. I've taken the back room there, and soundproofed it, and put the piano in there. It's been the most marvelous thing, because not only have I been able to do exactly that, but I can compose there, and I can do a little gardening, which I find is the most wonderful way to relax after a couple of hours of heavy work. I can just walk out into the garden, through the French doors—it's very small, including the whole flat—and grow things. Also I've started painting, so I've created a little area in my studio where I have my acrylics and my canvases. In the front part of my apartment, I have my computer where I've been writing. I've been doing my composition, also writing words. So this studio has enabled me to do at least three things that I wasn't able to do so well where I was. Of course, I could have sold the place there and moved way out in the countryside and bought a bigger place. But in many ways, it's wonderful to live in the city. It's important for me to be able to go to concerts and dance performances with ease. It's the sort of thing that if I did live two hours' drive outside, I probably wouldn't end up doing it. That's really what the MacArthur has enabled me to do, and that is something quite wonderful.

What types of subjects do you create in your paintings?
Well, I've been doing many layered abstract paintings. I've enjoyed working with colors and textures. I've only been doing it for two months. It's just the beginning of experimenting with things. You know, it's something that I've been enjoying with an absolute passion. I find, in fact, if anything, it's become a little bit distracting! I've been enjoying enormously doing that. I find not just that it's an artistic outlet. I love to think of music in terms, not just of color so much, but of texture. And I often think when I'm pedaling, and working out a different pedaling, of an equivalent transparency that you can find in the flesh tones, for instance, of a van Eyck, or an impressionist landscape where you see the color is solid, and yet somehow you see through it. So I've been experimenting with all those, and also with the immensely rich colors. I do feel that there is really a direct connection with playing.

The plant world opens that up as well, by looking at the colors of plants in different light, and in different parts of the world.
Absolutely. I do think that people underestimate how important this is. You know, we play the piano with our hands, but actually, the brain has 95 percent to do with what's going on. Anyone on the street can wiggle their fingers quickly in the air. It's the connection of where you put the fingers on the keys, and that has to do with the connection of good mental health and sort of open channels of creativity. It's a tremendously important thing and

I'm trying to create time, now more each year, to do these things. To write more, for example. I just had four weeks off and it was great. I was sketching a mass, and for the first time I could sit down for a whole day and actually write. Normally I grab a half an hour here and half an hour there between e-mails and dashing to the airport, practicing, and so on. It's so important for the freshness of what we do. I'm playing the Emperor Concerto this week. It's a piece that I've known for most of my life and played a lot of times. You know, how does one keep something like that fresh, so that every time you walk out onto the stage, you're shaking with the excitement to play it? That somehow the music is so thrilling and fresh. This is part of the skill of being any kind of performer on the stage, including an actor who is in a six-month run of a play. How do you still have the real tears you need to create when you're playing this role? It's the inner resources that have to be nourished and taken care of.

Yes, by doing other things in addition to your professional life, it tends to freshen you. It gives you a cleansing transition period. I want to ask you about audiences around the world today as compared with when you first started internationally in 1983 when you won the Naumburg. It's unbelievable to think that it was 23 years ago.
Yes. I don't like to think about it!

It does seem terrible to put it that way. How do you find that audiences have changed, or have they?
I'm not sure they have. I find that audiences every night are different in every city. It's never the same experience twice even if it's exactly the same people, which is obviously unlikely. We all come to a concert, you know, in a different mood, or wearing a different set of clothes. I don't think there are any rules about audiences. This is one of the reasons it's interesting. It is a creative part of a concert. I really felt that, for instance, when I was playing the *Ghost Variations* of George Tsontakis last week, or the week before, in Salzburg. You know, it's a big, 30-minute, American piece. It's not something that you would naturally think that a Salzburg audience would respond to. So I was a little bit worried. There are these Mozart variations in the middle that almost poke fun of Mozart. I worried that they might become restless or worse. But there was a tremendous concentration, a real sense of them listening and being involved. At the end there was an amazing reaction, which was thrilling. I felt that I was actually encouraged to play better during the performance, because I could sense that they were with me. Conversely, if you feel that the audience is restless, or bored, or reading their programs,

then you kind of get put off and you lose your concentration. Audiences have an active role to play. I think, though, the main differences in the last 25 years is that there are probably fewer recital series taking place in the world now, and hugely fewer than the 25 years before I started. It may be there's too much going on in people's homes, too many distractions.

Yes, that was one of my questions: How would you characterize the general health of the solo recital? There is not quite the interest there once was. Recitals are rarer now. It's rare to find a recital series—and not just piano, but a pianist with a singer, or a pianist with a violinist. Which is too bad.

There are still some very healthy ones, of course. There was a time when virtually every town would have a series. I suppose that one reason is that around the turn of the 20th century and up to the Second World War, so many people took piano lessons. It was the thing to do, especially for women. It was one of those skills like sewing or whatever. And so there was a ready audience. You would struggle at home with your Chopin nocturne, and then into town would come Rubinstein. You would want to go hear how a real pianist played it. There was this fascination with that. Now very few homes, in comparison, have pianos.

Yes, every home used to have one. Now it's the computer and the television.

And now there are fewer piano makers, except that there are quite a number in the Far East. Actually, I think that in the Far East there really is good health in many ways. Thank goodness for all those young Asian children who are having piano lessons, both in the West and at home.

Do you play frequently in Asia?

I go there about once a year or every 18 months. It's a long way to go unless you can make a little tour of it. Sometimes I can have a date offered by someone in Hong Kong and it doesn't work as the same period as a date in Tokyo, so I wouldn't go for just two concerts in Hong Kong. Next year my big trip is to Australia. I will drop in on Singapore on my way home and play there with the orchestra.

You've recently become an Australian citizen.

That was just an off-chance thing really, because my father was born there. I've always enjoyed going there. It's one of my favorite places to play and visit. On one trip someone mentioned to me that if my father had been born there it would be easy to get a passport. This lady actually looked into it for me and sent me these extraordinarily simple forms it took me no time to fill in. I sent off a copy of my passport and of my father's passport and 50 pounds, and in a couple of months back came a certificate saying that I was an Australian citizen! My grandfather ended up living there his whole life, and my father and he are both dead now. My decision to go ahead with the citizenship was prompted by a number of things. It was partly a filial tribute to two generations of my family who are now gone.

Do you think you may end up having a residence there?
I may very well in the future spend a couple of months a year there, and perhaps do some teaching. They've got a marvelous conservatorium in Sydney, and a gorgeous building. They built it underground, right into the very rocks on which the city is built, so the inner walls of a modern building are the very fabric of the country. It's a thrilling contrast! I like Australia very much. Well, it has many similarities to America, I suppose. I like the New World aspect of it, and the fact that the traditions are being created, rather than merely observed. I love the wine and the people and the food and the sun and the ocean . . . and it does no harm to have as many passports as you can. You never know when they could come in handy!

Yes, in today's world especially.
That, too.

You may need a hideout!
I think New Zealand probably would be more useful as a sort of avoidance of terrorists. I think Australia, sadly, is on the A-list, along with Britain and America and other places.

You believe very strongly that pianists and, I would suppose any other serious performing musician, should be composers, or transcribers, even though they are not going to write masterpieces, and they know it. You've pointed out that it's very important to be a creator. And along this line, in the last few years there are indeed more pianists, like you, than say, 25 or 50 years ago. You and Marc-André Hamelin and Mikhail Pletnev have shown amazing creativity in this area. Do you have any thoughts on why this is happening now?
I think we're coming out of a period of a sort of intellectual snobbery, in the '50s and '60s, but it really dates back a little earlier. There is a very interesting book that I found extremely interesting and provoking. It's John Carey's

The Intellectuals and the Masses,[5] which I would highly recommend. One of the points he makes is that after the First World War, a group arose (he was thinking mainly of writers) who had no interest in appealing to ordinary people. Indeed, they often had a real distaste for it. People like Joyce, Eliot, and Virginia Woolf. Part of what they wanted to do was to create this small group of like-minded intellectuals and play their own esoteric games with each other. Ezra Pound was also one of them. This is not to undermine the staggering achievements of what they did, but it often went hand-in-hand with a disdain for those who were not on the cutting edge with them.

They closed out the people who are not in that circle.
Yes, in fact Virginia Woolf was famously horrified when she thought some uneducated person enjoyed one of her books. It would have meant that it wasn't very good! This attitude was evident throughout the arts with modernism. And so, for those who didn't feel that they could create a masterpiece like *Ulysses*, they were intimidated at best, or actually discriminated against at worst.

So they didn't do anything.
Well, they either stopped writing altogether, or found it impossible to be published or promoted. Anyone who tried to compose nonserial music in the '50 and '60s would find it hard to get a performance. And not just that, but would be laughed at and thought to be old-fashioned. It was a very, very repressive age. I think it's ironic really because the '60s was such a liberated age in so many other ways. Who knows what great works we've lost because of the inability of people to leave space for many different kinds of artistic expression. In the late '70s, for all kinds of complicated social and political reasons, a change came about, and we've learned to enjoy much greater freedom since. And that includes the freedom to play and enjoy the great modernist masterpieces. I'm working on the Webern *Variations*, at the moment, which I adore. But I hope it doesn't mean that I can't also enjoy lighter, more romantic works.

It's wonderful that many of us have learned to enjoy once again these lighter, more romantic works. And this includes the transcriptions and paraphrases that you've been playing recently. I want to compliment you especially on your "Sleeping Beauty" paraphrase. It's a wonderful Lisztian tour de force! Do you offer it often as an encore?
I've not played it for a little while. I used to. During one season I was closing the program with it. I do often play something of my own as an encore.

I had a period when I, too, was intimidated and felt I had no talent to write original music, so all I allowed myself to do was to write some transcriptions. Actually, it was John Corigliano who heard one of these and really liked it. He said, "You should write some original music." I started thinking again about it. When I was younger I wrote much more. So now I am writing far fewer transcriptions than original pieces. I'm grateful to him for this.

Have you gotten on with the bassoon concerto?
I have, but it's undergone a transformation. I finished it, and I realized that most of the solo part would work better on the cello—it's the same range, of course. The piece became very tragic and expressive and seemed to suit the personality of the cello much more. This coincided with the fact that the bassoonist, who had originally asked me to write it, was out of touch, and the recording that was originally planned appeared to have fizzled out. I made a version for cello, and read it through with Steven Isserlis. He seemed to like it and said he'd like to play it. So we are doing it! It's getting its first performance in March in Liverpool next year.[6]

Is it called Cello Concerto, or does it have a name?
It's called *The Loneliest Wilderness, Elegy for Cello and Orchestra*. I wrote a song with words by Herbert Read inspired by the First World War. It's called "My Company," in which the officer, many years after the war, is thinking back to all the young men who died under his command. It has a feeling of overwhelming sadness and nostalgia as he remembers them. One of the lines of the poem is "the loneliest wilderness," hence the title.

We'll look forward to hearing this. I want to ask you about cadenzas. You are playing the Beethoven Fifth Concerto this weekend in Chicago. Are you playing your own cadenzas?
No, because Beethoven actually stops you from doing that by specifying the cadenza he wants you to play. I'm not sure in any Beethoven concerto I would play my own cadenzas. I think by that point the cadenza had become part of the composition, and indeed almost the most important part. If you think of the Fourth Concerto, the second cadenza is one of the most beautiful things in the whole piece. York Bowen wrote a quite lovely, lyrically romantic cadenza for Beethoven's Fourth, but it's more a curiosity than a possibility for modern performance, I think. With Mozart, sometimes you have to play your own cadenzas because often he wrote none himself.

You could use one written by someone else.
That seems to me a bit of a lost opportunity in a way. I think it is meant to be something of your own—ideally improvised, of course.

I gave this some thought after Garrick Ohlsson was taken to task recently for playing Badura-Skoda's cadenzas for Mozart's *Coronation* Concerto.[7] I thought, *Yes, Ohlsson could certainly play his own cadenzas.* In the end, what should a good cadenza do for the piece? Beethoven, as you say, pretty much takes care of that.
Yes, I think by Beethoven's time and beyond, the cadenza is written into the piece. One thinks of concertos such as the Tchaikovsky First, the Schumann, the Grieg, the Rachmaninoff Third, and above all, the Prokofiev Second—these cadenzas have become the emotional highlight, the climax of the whole piece. It's not just the time to decorate the final cadence, which is, of course, how it all began. It *is* the piece.

Although I was shocked recently when I heard a recording of Lars Vogt, the German pianist, playing Beethoven's First Concerto. He got to the first cadenza and it was this piece of music that had nothing to do with anything. I hadn't read the notes prior to listening, but it turned out to be Glenn Gould's cadenza.[8] The cadenza was a whole piece, totally modern, stuck right in here. Does that wake the audience up? It certainly woke me up!
I think there's a place for that kind of experiment, in a way. I did two, very modern cadenzas for Mozart concertos, and particularly in the C Minor, K. 491, I thought it was not at all "out of place." Mozart didn't write a cadenza for this piece, and to reach the climax of the first movement and have a watered-down Mozart-style cadenza seems to me like an anticlimax. It is better there to move aside from the style entirely and have something that takes the harmonic implications of the original and plays with them in a radical way. I also did a cadenza for K. 488 in a modern style, but I'm less convinced about that because the music is so utterly diatonic, unlike K. 491.

So the audiences should be able to get that?
Yes, cadenzas were traditionally done in the style of the time of performance rather than time of composition.

You've rather recently recorded the Swiss volume of Liszt's *Années de Pèlerinage*. Do you remember when you were first drawn to Liszt? Was that early on, or did that come later?

It did come a little later actually. I was under the total misconception, when I was very young, along with a lot of people, that Liszt was superficial. I much preferred Chopin to Liszt. I only knew the Hungarian Rhapsodies and pieces like that, as well as some of the études. So it did come later. My teacher Gordon Green actually edited a volume of Liszt and was very keen, particularly, on the late pieces. Actually, I think I can pinpoint my awakening to hearing Nyiregyházi playing the "Cypresses from the Villa d'Este." I found the recording in the Royal Northern College library when I was about 16. It really opened my eyes to a whole other side of Liszt, to this late style of this melancholic, spiritual, and tragic music. Then, of course, I heard the sonata around that same time. I remember finding that piece overwhelming, too. It was the British pianist Peter Donohoe playing it in Manchester. It was a very, very powerful experience to hear that for the first time.

Liszt isn't just one person. He's so multisided, with such a long life. One wonders constantly how he found the time to commit what he was doing at the piano to the written composition. Do you have plans for further recording of Liszt's music?
Nothing actually in the books. It's certainly something I'm always going to want to continue working on. I may at some point do the Italian *Pèlerinage*.

What about Saint-Saëns? How did you come to him?
When I was at Juilliard I got an offer to play the Fifth Concerto with the London Symphony Orchestra. Actually, it was going to be my first time playing with them, so it was an important concert. I would never have chosen this piece, but it had to be that piece or nothing, so I bought the score and started learning it. And I fell in love with it! It's been an extraordinary piece for me—almost like an old friend. I've played it so much. It's always been a good friend you look to. The Saint-Saëns Fifth always works because it's so well crafted.

Is that your favorite of the five?
I couldn't say which is my favorite. They're all so different. I certainly knew Two, Four, and Five, and I was thinking of recording those. But when I suggested it to Hyperion, they said, "Well, really, if you're going to do that, we'd like the complete works." I kind of rebelled for a little bit, but then I decided to go ahead with it.

We heard you in Madison in May play the Fourth with the Madison Symphony Orchestra under John DeMain, which was quite exciting. Saint-Saëns

is one of those composers who most musicians don't think a lot about. Yet he was so prolific. I wonder whether you have explored any of his solo works and would think about recording those some time.

The strange thing about Saint-Saëns is that the solo music is not really of the same stature as the chamber works or the concertos. He never wrote a sonata, for instance. They're mainly small pieces, and some of them are very nice. In fact, I'm going to be playing one of them next season on a program where the whole second half is waltzes. I'll play his "*Valse nonchalante*" on that program. I find that he's very interesting harmonically. Actually Lowell Liebermann was playing one of the violin sonatas recently and was saying how astonishing and how rich and colorful it is without any chromaticism. His music is very often just white notes, just pure diatonic writing, and yet he manages somehow to find these wonderful harmonic colors.

He's another very interesting character, too.
Yes. He traveled a lot.

There is the northern African influence there. You brought up Lowell Liebermann who wrote his Second Concerto for you and you have played John Corigliano's *Étude Fantasy*. Are there any other living composers you would really like to have a piece from, or would you like to have another piece from one of these?
Well, all is very possible. Certainly, George Tsontakis is someone who wrote me a piano concerto last year, which I recorded with the Dallas Symphony. That will be coming out on CD in the summer of 2007. It's a wonderful, huge, 40-minute work. The problem, I find, is just time. If I could learn quicker and didn't have other things to do, then I'd love to be learning new pieces all the time. But I really hate to learn things in a sketchy way. I have to learn any piece absolutely thoroughly. So this limits me to learning a certain number of pieces. So if I'm going to learn a 40-minute concerto, which is going to take me six months of intense work, I can't take a risk, and think, well, it might be a good piece. I've got to know before committing myself.

Do you think it's increasingly difficult for composers today to write ever-more imaginative music for the piano? Or are the possibilities still pretty much endless?
I suppose they're endless in a way. Of course, every piece that is written, like every doctoral thesis that is submitted, means that that can't be written

again. I suppose there is a finite end, though I don't think we've reached it yet. Composers are finding new things to say.

You spoke quite in depth with Elizabeth Haddon in the interview she did with you—which appeared in *Making Music in Britain* about your teach‐ ers. You spoke highly of Heather Slade-Lipkin who was all of 18 when you went to her. What do you remember specifically about her teaching?
Well, she's still teaching. She's a very, very thorough teacher. She gave me, you know, a very strict and good foundation on which to build—and that's everything. The first teachers we have are the most important. Later you gather from all sorts of sources—from teachers, from concerts, or from books. But the early years, when you're learning the basic technique about how to play the instrument, are so important. I'm conscious at the moment that near my apartment building in New York, they're building a new 40-story apartment block. It took them five times as long to build the foundation as it has been to put in the whole front façade. I owe Heather that in my piano playing.

You spoke so highly of your teacher Gordon Green, especially about the fact that he was a great human being who never sought to be famous. It's so important.
Yes, I think it's a problem if you enter teaching as a career to make you famous. There may be ambition alongside the dedication, but if it's at the forefront, I think the student's welfare could suffer. You have to realize that getting good, talented students is often a matter of luck. You have to do the best you can with every student you have. But I think there is an element in many music colleges of fierce competitiveness among teachers, and the students suffer for it.

It's really destructive. That makes me think of Adele Marcus of whom you spoke with Elizabeth Haddon. You were lucky not to have been pulled in, in a detrimental way, under her spell.
Yes. I really don't like talking about someone in that way, especially about someone who had a distinguished and long career. But I think my experi‐ ence with her, at the end of her life, was rather negative. Because I felt that all the things that I had admired so much in Gordon Green—his breadth, his openness, his willingness to have me do things differently from how he would do them, to let me have my own ideas—were totally different with Adele. She really seemed to want students to copy her: "This is how to play

it." I found it very claustrophobic. If I had stayed there another year I may not have been playing today.

You were not the only person she treated in this manner.
No. I was with her when I won the Naumburg. In fact, most of the things I played in the Naumburg we had not worked on at all. She didn't like the fact that I had won and said, "Oh, now we need to do a lot more work before you're ready to play." In fact, I had some debut recitals that came from the prize, and she was constructing the most ludicrous programs. I just know that if I had followed her advice, it would have all been a disaster. So I somehow had to try it out on my own and do it all by myself. I learned all of this repertoire—seven new concertos one season—and played it for nobody. I had to become self-sufficient very quickly. There were people studying with her who were huge talents, and I feel that maybe they didn't achieve all that they could because of the way she taught. She would also make many of them very nervous and neurotic about things, and I think that's terrible. We just need to feel very free about things. Be free to make mistakes, and be free to experiment. These are all things for which I'm so grateful for having had Gordon Green and Derrick Wyndham, my other teacher at the Royal Northern College of Music.

You played recently at the Hurstwood Farm Piano Studios[9] in England, where they have a variety of new instruments.
Yes. They have a number of interesting lines. They have the Australian Stuart and Sons piano. Richard Dain who runs the farm is an extraordinary man. At 80 years old, he's still inventing things for the piano. He's actually put together his own very impressive new design of piano which the Steingräber factory is building for him.

When you played there, were you given the choice of any piano you wanted to play?
Actually his new piano had just arrived, his Steingräber Phoenix. So I ended up playing that for the concert and that was very interesting. No, it's great that there are all these other makes around now, with the Stuart and the Fazioli. These are two very small concerns, both run by Mr. Fazioli and Mr. Stuart.

Do you have any personal feelings or leaning toward either of those?
I don't find any of these actually rival the Steinway. Although I find the Stuart is the most interesting because it's the most different from a Steinway.

Many of the other pianos around are trying to copy Steinway, and do similar kinds of things. Whereas the Stuart is actually a completely different design, and I actually find that interesting. In fact, they're quite wonderful. I've played them a number of times in Australia.

Have you tried the Fazioli?
I owned one. I bought one about three years ago, but I've since sold it. I think the Fazioli is an extraordinarily well-made instrument. But I just don't find, for myself, that its sound world is very interesting. I find it almost too clean, almost too clinical, and too perfect. They have this design feature where the duplex scaling is tuned exactly an octave higher than the note, which gives each note more clarity, but in some ways mere clarity isn't always a virtue if you want to create color, with overtones and half lights. There are pianists who love Faziolis, and I'm thrilled that there are piano makers around who are prepared to experiment and make absolutely first-rate instruments like Fazioli and Stuart.

It's very interesting that at the beginning of the 21st century, there are these different instruments, whereas 30 years ago when Fazioli started in the 1970s, we wouldn't have taken anything seriously but the Steinway. I want to move to another topic now. You've been a Hyperion recording artist for quite a few years. Do you have any particular thoughts on studio recordings as opposed to live performances?
Well, I think making a CD is like making a movie. You go in there with a certain image and vision, and try to create that in a permanent form, by whatever means, in the studio. The live performance is almost the exact opposite, because there you want to create something that is completely spontaneous—nonpermanent. This is one of the great skills involved in making a CD. Let's take the Liszt sonata. You can take the demonic aspect and go with that as the absolute principal voice of the whole piece. It can be thrilling in a concert situation. Or else you can take the angelic side of this piece and focus on that aspect. I think if you heard one of these one-sided facets on a recording more than once, you might feel that it was limited in scope—even contrived. In a recording I'm looking for a more all-rounded vision of the piece. Of course, the danger is almost that it just sounds middle of the road. That is where the challenge comes in—to create a frisson as well as a sense of stature and record.

So that someone would be eager to go back to that recording. Have you released a live solo recital performance to date?
Not a live solo, no.

Just the Rachmaninoff concertos.
And also the Beethoven violin sonatas many years ago with Robert Mann. Those were recorded live in concert.

Do you have any particular recording that you're most proud of?
As a whole CD? Well, probably the Rachmaninoff set. I'm pleased with the way the whole thing turned out and sounds, including the magnificent orchestral playing and actual piano sound. As a solo record, I think the Mompou is one of my favorites.

That's the first CD of yours that I really got to know and I'm very fond of it. It's interesting because some don't find it engaging, because the music is so delicate.
It's interesting because I know some of Mompou's solo recordings, with himself playing. He has no technique as far as fingers whatsoever, but he is a virtuoso. He's a virtuoso of sound. And that's one of the things that I think I was looking for in that CD. It's just that when people think of a big technique, they automatically think of playing quickly, but actually, to me a technique doesn't even leave the starting post until it's involved with color and pedaling, too.

Actually you sent me to buy a volume of Mompou's music. I love those harmonies that are slightly different each time a chord is repeated. It's all very subtle. Were you in contact at all with Wilfrid Mellers when you were preparing that CD?
I wasn't in contact. I never met him. He actually sent me an extremely warm letter after the CD was released. He wrote a lovely book on Mompou[10] and he told me that he would incorporate some of my ideas when it was republished in paperback. He's very, very elderly.

My husband and I got to know him rather well when he held a visiting professorship at the University of Alabama in the spring of 1987, after he retired from the University of York. I first met him in York when I was doing a biography of Egon Wellesz, with whom Mellers had studied. He didn't want to talk about Wellesz, but rather the music of the American South because I am from the South. He's always been interested in American music. I've admired all of Mellers's works, including the book on Mompou. Then you made this recording. You recently played a Mompou piece as an encore after the Saint-Saëns Fourth Concerto in Madison.
Yes, I often play Mompou as an encore.

Just a week preceding your performance, Leif Ove Andsnes also played one of Mompou's pieces as an encore after his recital at the Schubert Club in St. Paul. How often is one going to hear Mompou offered as an encore one week after the other? That's been a wonderful experience! I'm going to change the subject considerably here. Do you have any particular way you handle the physical stresses of travel?

Well, I'm very lucky that I sleep well. Maybe one day a year do I have any kind of insomnia, where I would wake up and not be able to go instantly back to sleep. This is a fantastic gift. I have colleagues, friends, who have awful jet-lag problems. They have nights where they don't sleep at all and have to get up the next morning and have a rehearsal. That must be a real curse. I also have a pretty good stomach. I can eat different foods. What do I do? Well, I think a lot has to do with mental health, and the ability to let go, as well as the ability to have, if you like, a contemplative, spiritual view of life, which I do. I'm a Catholic. It's an important part of my life. In a sense, it puts other things into perspective, reminding me to return always to thinking about the bigger picture. Also I do a little bit of working out, I suppose. A little bit on the exercise machine as I was doing earlier today. Not very much, but just enough to keep things ticking. I walk a lot. I would walk rather than take the car. So those are a few things that come to mind.

And you yourself teach, don't you?

Not regularly. I go into the Royal Academy of Music in London sporadically and I do master classes probably two or three times a year. I've actually got a position there, as a visiting professor, but I do very, very little. I like doing it when I can.

Aren't you also connected to the Royal Northern College of Music?

That, too. They asked me if I would take up the International Chair of Piano Studies. The problem is that it is 200 miles north, so it's a little bit difficult. I was just trying to find a date this week to visit. That's my old school, and I'm very fond of it. I'm happy to have this position if they don't mind my habitual unavailability! Who knows, I may be able to do more in the future.

Are you able to generalize about where the best emerging young pianists are coming from in the world today?

Well, it's a bit difficult. There are some very good ones coming from the academy where I teach. What I like there is that they've got a tremendous free attitude toward teaching. Christopher Elton is head of piano there. I think it's a remarkable situation because there will be students who he will happily send to play for another teacher on the faculty if he feels there is something to be gained. For instance, if the student is playing Medtner, Hamish Milne is teaching there, and he's one of the great Medtner experts and has recorded a lot of his music. He wouldn't hesitate to say, "Go and play this for Hamish." That kind of thing, to me, is just wonderful. I hear a number of students from there and I find that each of them plays differently. To me, that's the best sign of a school, or a studio. Every student has been given the space to have his own personality. You can't ask more than that. You can't create a great artist, but you can certainly destroy one. I remember the great French novelist Julian Green, who taught English for a while at the University of Virginia, writing that if a student of his left university and still wanted to read, he considered that to be good teaching. All you can do in the end is make people enthusiastic about the subject at hand, thirsty to keep reading, and curious. Because most of what we learn, we learn when we leave school anyway.

Exactly. You're just taught how to go about learning, and that is the most important thing. You spoke somewhere about the aspect of breathing and how very important it is for everyone, and especially for musicians to sing, on the breath. Music is on the breath. Can you clarify your thoughts on how it is important for both the composer and the performer to sing so that your listeners can leave the hall having heard music and have that sense of singing?
Well, it is just that composers are human beings and breathing is about the most fundamental thing any of us do, so it would be very unnatural in the creation of music if breathing has somehow disappeared. You know, I think it's interesting about song and dance. Those are the foundation of all music. That's where it all comes from—this urge to sing and this urge to dance. We all have it in us. We were talking about creating things. You go into a school for young people and they're all encouraged to express themselves with finger paint. Why is it that this is suddenly not done when we leave school, or even when we get into high school?

One becomes self-conscious.
So I think it's this natural quality of instinct, really, that we need to recover in music. So often, folk musicians are so much more natural with this than classical musicians. They allow things to just be. I'm not advocating, of course, a totally discipline-less way. To play an instrument well, I think you need an enormous amount of discipline to have technique, but also let's not

lose sight of certain basic things. This rhythmic exuberance that you see in dancing is important.

We should take care to cultivate the whole spirit of that in ourselves every day!
Yes.

I want to thank you so much for taking this hour to share your thoughts. You've said important things that all musicians should think about, and not just musicians, but people who are your audience as well. As well, thank you for reviving so much music that has a simple charm.

Select Discography

Bis
W. A. Mozart. Quintet in E-flat Major, K. 452; Adagio in C Minor and Rondeau in C Major, K. 617. Beethoven. Quintet in E-flat Major, op. 16. With the Berlin Philharmonic Wind Quintet. Bis-CD-1552. 2007.

Chandos
Johann Nepomuk Hummel. Concerto # 2 in A Minor, op. 85; Concerto # 3 in B Minor, op. 89. English Chamber Orchestra. Bryden Thomson, conductor. *Gramphone* Award for Concerto Recording of the Year. 1987.

Hyperion
Frederic Chopin. *Late Masterpieces*. Sonata in B Minor; *Berceuse*; *Barcarolle*; *Polonaise-Fantasy*; Nocturnes; Mazurkas. CDA67764. 2010.

Peter I. Tchaikovsky. Three *Pianos Concertos; Concert Fantasia. The Romantic Concerto*, vol. 50. Minnesota Orchestra. Osmo Vänskä, conductor. Two discs. CDA 67711/2. 2010.

A *Mozart Album*. W. A. Mozart. *Fantasia* in C Minor, K. 475; Sonata in B-flat Major, K. 333; *Fantasia* in C Minor, K. 396/385f; Johann Baptist Cramer. *Hommage à Mozart*; Ignaz Friedman. *Menuetto* in D Major. Hough. Three Mozart Transformations (after Poulenc); Franz Liszt/Ferruccio Busoni. *Fantasia on Two Themes from The Marriage of Figaro*. CDA 67598. 2008.

George Tsontakis. *Man of Sorrows* for piano and orchestra. Dallas Symphony Orchestra. Andrew Litton, conductor. Live recording from 2005. Arnold Schoenberg. *Sechs kleine Klavierstücke*, op. 19; Alban Berg. Piano Sonata; Anton Webern. *Variations for Piano*, op. 27; Tsontakis. *Sarabesques*. CDA 67564. 2007.

Stephen Hough's Spanish Album. Various Spanish, French, and other composers, including Hough. CDA 67565. 2006.

The Stephen Hough Piano Collection. Shorter selections of various works, including his own *Suite Osmanthus* and Earl Wild's virtuosic transcription of a "Pas de quatre" from Tchaikovsky's ballet music. 2005.

Sergei Rachmaninoff. Four Piano Concertos; *Rhapsody on a Theme of Paganini.* Dallas Symphony Orchestra. Andrew Litton, conductor. Two discs. CDA 67501/2. 2004.

Stephen Hough's English Piano Album. Includes works by Alan Rawsthorne, Stephen Reynolds, York Bowen, Frank Bridge, and Hough's two "*Valses enigmatiques.*" Hough contributed the liner notes to this recording. CDA 67267. 2002.

Camille Saint-Saëns. *The Complete Works for Piano and Orchestra. The Romantic Concerto,* vol. 27. City of Birmingham Symphony Orchestra. Sakari Oramo, conductor. Two discs. CDA 67331/2. 2001. *Gramophone* Gold Disc Award in 2008, presented in honor of the most popular classical CD over the past 30 years.

Stephen Hough's New Piano Album. Various composers, including Hough. CDA 67043. 1999.

New York Variations. John Corigliano. *Étude Fantasy;* Aaron Copland. *Piano Variations;* Ben Weber. *Fantasia (Variations);* George Tsontakis. *Ghost Variations.* CDA 67005. 1998.

Frederico Mompou. *Piano Music.* CDA 66963. 1997.

Franz Xaver Scharwenka. Piano Concerto # 4 in F Minor, op. 82. Emil von Sauer. Piano Concerto # 1 in E Minor. *The Romantic Piano Concerto,* vol. 11. City of Birmingham Symphony Orchestra. Lawrence Foster, conductor. CDA 66790. 1995. *Gramophone* Award for Record of the Year, and Concerto Recording of the Year. First recording of both of these concertos.

Notes

1. Elizabeth Haddon, *Making Music in Britain: Interviews with Those behind the Notes* (Burlington, VT: Ashgate, 2006), 105.

2. *Suite R-B,* as well as other compositions and transcriptions by Hough, are published by Josef Weinberger.

3. Ben Summerskill, ed., *The Way We Are Now: Gay and Lesbian Lives in the 21st Century* (London: Continuum, 2006).

4. Introduced by Nicolas Kenyon (London: Continuum, 2007).

5. John Carey, *The Intellectuals and the Masses: Pride and Prejudice among the Literary Intelligentsia, 1880–1939* (London: Faber & Faber, 1992).

6. Hough conducted the Royal Liverpool Philharmonic Orchestra in this premiere.

7. Allan Kozinn, "Mozart's Loftiest in an Intimate Setting at Lincoln Center," *The New York Times,* 3 Aug. 2006.

8. Glenn Gould's cadenzas for Beethoven's First Concerto were written in 1954 and are heard on Lars Vogt's recording with Simon Rattle and the City of Birmingham Orchestra, recorded in 1995. EMI Classics, 2002.

9. Sevenoaks, Kent.

10. Wilfrid Mellers, *Le Jardin retrouvé: The Music of Frederic Mompou (1893–1987)*, limited edition (York, England: Fairfax Press, 1989). Mellers died at age 94 in May of 2008.

Steven Osborne. Photo by Ben Ealovega

CHAPTER SIX

~

Steven Osborne

Steven Osborne was born in 1971, and grew up in Linlithgow, Scotland, in a home where music played a large part. While his musical training took place solely in Britain, he came to wider recognition after winning the Clara Haskil Competition in Switzerland in 1991, and later the Naumburg International Piano Competition in New York in 1997.

The Naumburg award brought forth his recording of Ravel's music for the Musical Heritage Society in 2000. He has been with Hyperion, however, since 1998 with his first recording of concertos by Alexander Mackenzie and Donald Tovey. Osborne has released many recordings, becoming widely known for his playing of the music of Debussy, Messiaen, Liszt, Rachmaninoff, Tippett, Britten, and Ravel. His recordings of Messiaen's *Vingt regards sur l'enfant-Jésus* and Tippett's complete piano music both earned significant recording awards. His accounts of Britten's works for piano with orchestra became the *Gramophone* award winner in 2009 in the concerto category.

Recording, however, is only one aspect of Osborne's musical activities. In diverse venues throughout Britain, the major cities of Europe and beyond, he has become equally known for his chamber music appearances, his role as a concerto soloist, and as a solo recitalist. In addition to being a frequent guest at London's Wigmore Hall, he appears regularly at the Edinburgh Festival. His concerto appearances at the BBC Proms have included performances of Tippett's concerto in 2005, Britten's concerto in 2007, and Rachmaninoff's First Concerto in 2010. His concert schedule takes him all around the world.

Osborne eagerly collaborates with like-minded musicians. He thus devotes much time playing chamber music with musicians from his own generation. With the British pianist Paul Lewis he shared numerous duet recitals of Schubert's music, including a performance at Wigmore Hall early in 2010, which culminated in a universally praised recording. Earlier, Osborne worked with the pianist Martin Roscoe in their acclaimed recording of Messiaen's *Visions de l'amen* for two pianos. He has frequently performed with his personal friend the German cellist Alban Gerhardt, and together they collaborated for two Hyperion recordings. In 2008 he played sonatas by Debussy, Prokofiev, and Brahms with the young Scottish violinist Nicola Benedetti. He and the German baritone Dietrich Henschel presented selections from Schubert's *Schwangengesang* and several Wolf lieder at Wigmore Hall in January of 2009.[1]

As a concerto soloist, Osborne has worked with the Royal Philharmonic, the BBC Symphony, the City of Birmingham Symphony, the BBC Scottish Symphony Orchestra, the Royal Scottish National Orchestra, the London Philharmonic Orchestra, Berlin Symphony, Deutsches Sinfonieorchester, Munich Philharmonic, Finnish Radio Symphony, Australian Chamber Orchestra, the NHK Symphony, and the Dallas Symphony Orchestra. Notable conductors with whom he has collaborated include Vladimir Ashkenazy, Alan Gilbert, Donald Runnicles, Yan Pascal Tortelier, Lief Segerstam, Andrew Litton, Stéphane Denève, Esa-Pekka Salonen, Vladimir Jurowski, Evgeny Svetlanov, and the late Sir Charles Mackerras.

During his career, Osborne's penchant for improvisation, which was early influenced by the American pianist Keith Jarrett, has been a steady influence on his musical life. Because he finds its benefits for his own playing are enormous, he has become an advocate of its benefits for all musicians, especially those classically trained. At one point he took a year off from learning new classical repertoire in order to reenergize himself through focusing solely on improvising.

In occasional writings found on his website, www.stevenosborne.com, Osborne delivers a fresh honesty about music, including his thoughts on approaching difficult musical works. For example, in 2010 while preparing to record Ravel's complete solo works, he was not hesitant to express his thoughts on Ravel's writing: "Nothing Ravel wrote is easy, even the pieces which sound it."

At the piano, Osborne sits far from the keyboard and can become a study in lively movement during a performance. While playing Mussorgsky's *Pictures at an Exhibition* in St. Paul, Minnesota, many of his listeners feared he would slip from the bench as it slowly moved backward during his active performance.

Osborne is married to the American clarinetist Jean Johnson who has a busy freelance schedule playing the orchestral, chamber music, and solo repertoire. Osborne and Johnson appeared together in recital throughout the country in the spring of 2010.

I spoke by telephone with Osborne at his home in Linlithgow on the 29th of August in 2008.

Interview

How long have you been back in Linlithgow, where you grew up?
I've been back here about eight years now. I studied in Manchester and stayed on there for several years until I started thinking about buying a house. Scotland seemed to be the obvious place. When you travel a lot, it's very helpful to be in a familiar place, where you feel at home. When I moved back to Scotland, I was surprised to suddenly find myself very happy. I wasn't aware that I'd felt unsettled before.

Was music a part of your very early life?
Both my parents played piano and my dad played organ, a freelance for church services. We had a piano in the house. My parents used to play piano duets together, and they played a lot of records in the house. I was probably about four when I started fiddling about on the piano. I've got one brother, Kenneth, who was a cellist and a wonderful musician, but he developed some problems with his arms while at music college which limited his study. He retrained as an accountant and is currently the finance director of the Royal Scottish National Orchestra.

Do you remember some of the pianists you listened to on recordings while you were young at home?
I do remember the *Moonlight* Sonata, and Beethoven's *Pastoral* Symphony but don't remember the artists. It wasn't until I was in my teens that I began to pay attention to particular pianists.

Did you hear pianists in recital, or in concerto performances, during your young years in Edinburgh?
Yes, lots. The ones I particularly remember are Ashkenazy, Bolet, and Arnaldo Cohen.

Was either your mother or your father your first teacher, or did you begin with someone else?
When I was about six I went to Sheila McCullough. For a year before that I went to one of her pupils.

What do you remember about your first lessons with McCullough?
I don't really remember how Sheila taught. I've been told that I wasn't good at reading music and liked to play by ear, so I would get her to play a new piece, and watch surreptitiously. Apparently I knew which note was which on the page but didn't know what octave to play them at. Once she got wind of that, she stopped demonstrating and made me work it out for myself. So she must have been a good teacher!

Yes. But on the other hand, it is so good to have an ear!
My dad is a natural musician and has a good ear. He improvises a bit, and when he does, it is very expressive. So if there's any question of heredity, it probably comes down through him. When I was 10 I went as a dayboy to St. Mary's Music School in Edinburgh and studied with Richard Beauchamp.[2] There were normal school subjects there but the big emphasis was music, with practice being timetabled into one's school day. Going to St. Mary's was probably the single most important factor in my development as a musician, being around like-minded people in a close community: there were only 40 pupils at that time. I felt very much at home.

Tell me about your study with Richard Beauchamp.
I remember that he had a horror of mindless technical exercises. He is a very idealistic man and very inquisitive musically. I remember one lesson on the Berg sonata in which the entire time was spent on just the first bar. I was beside myself because I couldn't get what he was talking about! He could be very provocative that way when he was trying to encourage you to think about music differently. He was a very inspiring man for me, and he's still teaching at the school.

He focuses a lot on healthy piano playing today. Was he concerned about this aspect of playing when you were with him some 25 years ago?
Yes, but I think he subsequently became more focused on it. There was one thing which I still use very much today. When you've got a relentless passage which is very tiring technically, you have to find a way to divide it up in your mind with imaginary moments of relaxation, even though physically your fingers don't have time to relax. But just the tiniest little thing in your mind

can help enormously. In general, he was very interested in experimenting to find the most efficient way of playing, and that has become an increasing preoccupation of mine in recent years; when I practice, I try to be constantly aware of any unnecessary tension in my body.

One thing that helped me greatly was Alexander Technique, which everyone had to do at St. Mary's. I didn't pay much attention to it at the time, but subsequently I've used it a lot, especially in the last couple of years when I've struggled with physical tension through being at the piano a great deal. So I've had to quite carefully examine how I sit at the piano, how I use my arms and fingers, where I get most tense. I also do Tai Chi, which is very helpful. Sadly, the physical aspects of playing are often neglected in instrumental teaching. It's much easier to solve problems when the bad habits are being formed than to undo them 20 years later.

I had a wonderful head of music at St. Mary's, Nigel Murray, who was a very forward-thinking man. He was the one who introduced Alexander Technique to the school. He had been a violinist but had to stop playing through injury so his interest in healthy playing had a very personal dimension. He would encourage us to think about what we were doing in a larger context, getting us to discuss issues like: "Rank these in order of importance: the composer, the score, the performer, the audience." I still think that's a great question. Every year, the school would perform one of the Bach Passions at Easter, and I'll never forget the year when he played the violin solo in "Erbarme dich" from the *St. Matthew Passion*—one of the most beautiful and heartbreaking things I ever heard. He didn't have full control of the instrument, but what he communicated was so human and vulnerable.

At what age did you realize music was going to be a major part of your life?
I don't remember this, but my mum told me that when I was seven I told her that I couldn't live without playing the piano. As far as I'm aware, I never actually thought in terms of what I was going to do for a living. Even when I went to music college, I wasn't thinking "Okay, I'm hoping to become a pianist." Then when I was 20, in 1991, I won the Clara Haskil Competition. That got me some concerts, and things gradually started to develop. I consider myself very lucky because I know how hard it can be to make a career for yourself even when you're minded to make it happen.

Did Beauchamp recommend Renna Kellaway[3] as a teacher at Manchester for you?
Not directly. When I was about 15 he told my parents he thought he was getting to the end of what he could teach me and suggested I go to someone

else to get a different kind of input. They made some inquiries, and Renna Kellaway was suggested. While I was still at school in Edinburgh, I went down to Manchester every couple of weeks for a lesson, and then continued with her when I went to music college in Manchester a couple of years later. Her approach was completely different from Richard's, much more based around technical exercises and finger strength. I was rather resistant at first, but I gradually started to see that it was useful. And I realize now that it was essential. I absolutely needed it, although it was a painful adjustment to make at the time. Idealism only gets you so far; your fingers have to work, too.

Did she bring much of her own South African background to her teaching?
Actually her musical background was very much a European one. She studied with Johannes Rôntgen and Franz Osborn[4] in Amsterdam and also had some lessons with Clara Haskil. Her style of playing was very much like that of Clara Haskil, with a focus on clarity, vocal line, and structure. When I first went to her I was overly reliant on the pedal; I loved that kind of resonance. Renna forced me to clean everything up and make all details count. With her I did a lot of Bach, Mozart, Schubert, and Beethoven.

Did she also stress the physical aspects of playing like Beauchamp?
Not to the extent that Richard did. She was more from the school of thinking that if something was hurting, you basically played through it. That gradually started to change while I was studying with her because several piano students of various teachers at the RNCM [Royal Northern College of Music] got injured. But in many cases, she was right. It's easy to be paranoid about every little ache and pain, and important to learn what the various aches mean. Some require care and rest, but many will go away by themselves.

Tell me about the camaraderie at the Royal Northern College. What kind of environment were you in with your fellow students?
Ah, it was absolutely fantastic! I had so many great friends there. A lot of that was helped by the fact that Manchester is a much smaller city than, for example, London. It's very easy to go to other people's houses. Not many of us had cars so we just cycled around. Many of these are still friends of mine, and they're teaching and playing today.

Do you remember anything about the kinds of instruments you and the other students were playing on then?
Many of the pianos at college were pretty clapped out, which is par for the course in most music institutions. There was a particular day when you could book practice rooms for the next week, and people would queue up outside

the college at five in the morning, even in the rain, in winter, so they could get the best pianos. I just thought that was completely ridiculous! I never did it, and spent much of my time practicing on Danemann uprights. I have a solid but unremarkable Kawai piano at home now because I don't think it helps to always practice on great pianos. A mediocre piano makes you work much harder to get the right sound. But of course, you do need some experience on good pianos, to discover what they are capable of. The problem is, though, if you've got a great piano at home, then have to perform on a bad one, it's very easy to get focused on the inadequacies of the instrument rather than on what you're playing. I think you need a mind-set where you're not focused on the piano. There are three situations where I really pay attention to what kind of piano I have: when I need something really loud, as with Rachmaninov concertos; when I'm playing repertoire that needs exceptionally fine control, for example, the Schubert B-flat Sonata; or when I'm recording. In this last case, I go to choose the piano a few months in advance to make sure I've got something suitable. In the other cases, sometimes the piano isn't up to scratch, but what can you do then? Best not think about it too much and just throw yourself into the music as fully as you can.

Are you familiar with Fazioli?
Yes, but I don't think I've come across the best of them. To be honest, I'm not really wrapped up in the whole question of pianos. You can get good pianos, and bad pianos, and sometimes great pianos. But I think for the audience it is not enormously significant. As an audience member, I think you relate everything to a certain average level of volume and brightness in the sound that gets established quite quickly, and after that it's much more about the performer's musical ideas than the precise sound of the instrument. You can basically get your musical ideas across on most instruments. Some composers are more delicate than others in this respect; I find the difference between a good and great piano for Schubert is very significant, for example.

You won the Clara Haskil Competition in 1991 and a few years later, in 1997, you won the Naumburg in New York.
Yes, both were useful for getting concerts, but a fringe benefit of the Naumburg was getting to know Bobby Mann,[5] who used to be first violinist of the Juilliard String Quartet. I've never met anyone who has so much insight about musical mind games, about how to be uninhibited in performance. By character I'm rather reserved, and inevitably that seeps into the music. I know that Bobby has always respected my playing, but he made a comment after one of my concerts that everything was so much in its place that there seemed no room for wildness or spontaneity. I thought a lot about that.

There can be much to admire in different ways of playing which are not particularly spontaneous, but I think what creates a visceral connection with the audience, and with yourself, is when you're not planning exactly what you're going to do, when you give yourself up to the music. It's a tricky thing to open up to if it's not instinctive, and takes a lot of time. I still feel I'm finding my way with that.

How do you feel about competitions?
They're very stressful to do, but they can be useful. If you can play well under that kind of stress it really strengthens you for whatever concerts you have to do. But it's a mistake to read too much into the results, win or lose. I've won competitions and I've been knocked out in the first round of others. I heard a great story about the very distinguished British pianist John Lill[6] who was once on the jury of the Leeds Competition. After the first round results were announced with all the competitors and jurors present, he stood up and gave an impromptu speech saying he deplored the results. He remarked that it's the nature of competitions that anyone with individuality generally gets voted out early because some jurors don't like their approach. People who play competently and inoffensively tend to advance. That's a problem that competitions will probably never overcome.

Have you ever served as a judge?
Only in really small competitions. The idea of doing a competition that takes two weeks or more doesn't appeal to me at all, partly because of the time commitment and partly because I can't imagine how one could listen with fresh ears for that long. Probably it's also a touch of cowardice. I know how much it means to all of those competitors and how disappointed many of them will be. It's a brutal system.

You are particularly associated with 20th-century composers. Is that the area of repertoire where you feel most comfortable?
Actually, it has always been important to me to have a very broad repertoire and not to specialize in any one area. Otherwise, it's like eating steak every day. I find that all the different areas of repertoire inform the others, and make me able to feel the music more richly. I've gone through different phases—at college I played a great deal of pre-romantic music, then in my later 20s I moved strongly into the romantic repertoire. Different composer obsessions come and go: Rachmaninov, Ravel, Messiaen, Tippett, and always Beethoven. In terms of what I play in concert, the thing that comes up most is probably Mozart concertos.

I want to talk about your recording label, Hyperion. They have the best technology available and promote the best performers. Let's talk about working with Hyperion and its recording process. First of all, do you like the recording process?

I love it now although it used to make me very stressed. The first thing is to give up the idea you can make a perfect record. No matter how well you play, a year later you'll wish you'd done many things differently. The less I try to control how I'm going to play the pieces for a recording, the more I like the results. As for Hyperion, they are great to work with. Everyone who works there loves music. It feels like we share the same values, and I think there is mutual respect. One reason it's nice to work with them is that they will commit to ideas which are difficult to market, but artistically strong, like the complete Tippett piano music, which I recorded a few years ago. They knew that I felt very strongly about Tippett's music, so they went ahead with it even though they knew they'd probably lose money on the project. And they did; they still didn't regret it!

This is Messiaen's centenary year and you're playing his music since you have a strong affinity for it. Do you remember when you first became aware of his music?

Yes, I was doing a summer music course in Edinburgh with Kenneth van Barthold, and one of his students there did some Messiaen pieces. I remember being rather interested in the sound world, but I didn't immediately love them. A few years later I learned a group of the *Vingt regards* and played them in a concert, and was really surprised by the fantastic response I got. I was rather expecting people to say, "Oh, modern music . . . oh, no," but it was clear that the music communicated very directly. I continued learning the *Vingt regards* bit by bit. It's a big project involving 20 pieces that take over two hours to perform. In the end, I was galvanized to finish them when Renna engaged me to do the whole thing at her music festival. I think she figured I'd never get around to finishing them off, and that gig forced me over the hump. That couple of months of learning was really tough, but I'm so glad I did it. It's an amazing piece to do in concert, in impact and intention not unlike a Bach Passion.

For all its compositional complexity, I find Messiaen's music wonderfully direct in its emotional world. He tends to use big blocks of material in which not much changes. There are a lot of juxtapositions rather than organic development, and the number of interpretive decisions you have to make are relatively few: the music almost plays itself once you make some basic decisions about tempo and character. And yet what he manages to express can be utterly overwhelming.

Did you ever have the chance to meet Messiaen?
No, I didn't, but I did play for his wife, Yvonne Loriod, in Paris a few years ago. She is an amazing character, as fresh after six hours of teaching as when she started. I'm reminded of several stories Paul Crossley told me about Messiaen. He had studied with Messiaen and he told me that Messiaen's only luxury was caviar; the fridge was full of it, supposedly. Another story was about an experience he had when he did Messiaen's composition class at the conservatoire. The whole of the first class consisted of Messiaen's reading the rules for the conservatoire! Maybe I've exaggerated the story in remembering it, but I think it reveals something of his essentially humble attitude.

You were nominated for a *Gramophone* Award for your well-received recording of Tippett's complete piano music. These works are highly difficult, very strong, muscular music. In your liner notes you wrote that the sonatas exhibit many of the elements found in Beethoven's music, for example, a strong engagement with conflict. Do you remember when you were first introduced to these pieces?
Yes, it was through Ian Kemp, my tutor at Manchester University. He wrote the program notes for that CD, incidentally. I took a course of his on Tippett's late music, not because I was particularly interested in the subject but because I loved Ian's teaching. I knew a couple of Tippett's early pieces but not his later music, and in fact, I was rather perplexed by it at first. Gradually I came to love it, but it's idiosyncratic, occasionally not on the highest level of inspiration, sometimes even mystifying. If you can forgive these things, the music brings enormous rewards. Tippett shares with Beethoven a robust attitude to conflict. For me, Beethoven always embraces conflict and finds a way to work through it to create something of beauty and strength; it is exactly the same with Tippett. That complete engagement with conflict is something that I find very moving. The Third Sonata of Tippett has a "resolution" which seems to be the product of sheer effort of will. On the other hand, the Fourth Sonata ends with a complex sense of resignation and acceptance.

What are your thoughts about a composer like Tippett, who had only modest abilities as a pianist, and yet created these difficult works for the instrument?
He wrote very badly for the piano. It's really hard on the hands, and that's highly irritating. But then that awkwardness is sometimes integral to the effect of the music.

Are you careful about your audience when you program his music?
To some degree. But then, if I were really careful I would never have programmed Tippett's music at all. If you believe in music which is very seldom
played, I would almost say it's a duty to program it. But that's the wrong word
because I love playing it. If I didn't have to think about the audience, I'd
probably play him on every other concert. But there are simple practicalities
beyond what an audience might be ready for—his music takes a lot of time
to prepare. Often there simply isn't the time.

Did you ever meet Tippett?
No. It's something I'm rather sad about.

Did you work with Paul Crossley[7] while working on Tippett's music?
I've not worked with him, but I met him and had a long chat.

What about Kapustin?
Yes, really fun stuff! That was a complete accident. I was playing snooker
with a friend who had a CD of the Second Sonata on in the background,
and I was very attracted to its strong synthesis of classical and jazz traditions.
I managed to get in touch with the performer on that CD, Nicolai Petrov,[8]
who arranged for someone to bring some of Kapustin's music over from Moscow because it wasn't published at that time in the U.K. And that's another
thing about Hyperion: I phoned them up and said I'd found this composer
Kapustin and asked if I could do a record. They asked, "What's the music
like?" I played two bars on the phone and the response was, "Yes, let's do it."
No exaggeration.

**That's a wonderful story. That quickly! It's music that is in a class of its
own. Marc-André Hamelin recorded another full CD which I knew before
yours. Will there be another recording of Kapustin's music perhaps from
you or someone else?**
I won't do another one; I don't know about Marc. Kapustin is a very prolific
composer and you really have to sift through the works. Every composer has
his clichés, but with Kapustin these clichés sometimes become a bit domi-
nant. But there are some wonderful pieces.

Did you meet him when he was in London?
No, I was in the States at that time, teaching improvisation at the University
of Connecticut.

What was the single most interesting thing you learned about the students you worked with?

The way they improvise is such a transparent reflection of their character. It's fascinating. In classical music you can hide behind the composer's notes. It's almost the orthodox view that a performer should not impose their own character on the music but let the composer speak through them. I think that's a very damaging notion, actually. I think the only way to serve the composer is to feel the music, and that must be profoundly subjective. One should certainly greatly respect the music, but also recognize that as a performer you must impose a great deal on the music to create an interpretation: There is so little information in a written score. It's a partnership between the score and one's emotions, and that balance is not simple to achieve. But the point about improvisation is, it's much harder to hide when you improvise, when you're starting from nothing or from a very elementary structure; often what comes out is a perfect reflection of someone's character, whether it be extrovert, shy, angry, peaceful, whatever. It's very much about being unguarded. In order for improvising to work, you have to be willing not to control it. You really have to go into it not knowing what's going to happen. It's a fascinating, wonderful experience when you put yourself into that mind-set and simply play what comes spontaneously. But to get to that point can be complicated; classical musicians are so used to self-censorship. In my opinion, improvising is just about the healthiest thing a musician can do. The more one experiences a true sense of spontaneity while improvising, the more it seeps into one's playing of the classical repertoire.

Has your own improvising led you to compose?

Yes, I have done a bit of composition, but it is much less interesting to me than my improvising. My composition is generally very derivative.

Are you engaged with any of the music of the younger generation of British composers?

I particularly like Julian Anderson's music.[9] I find that Julian has a beautiful ear for texture and structure. There's something very spontaneous about the way he structures his pieces that I like a lot. There is a certain kind of inevitability that becomes apparent as the piece progresses. It takes some surprising turn and you feel, "Oh, yes, of course."

Let's talk about collaboration and the art of making musical compromises with other performers. You frequently perform music with quite a few prominent, younger-generation musicians today.

I had an amazing experience with the Jerusalem Quartet when I first did the Shostakovich Quintet with them. It was immediately clear we had radically different ideas about how to play the piece: I wanted to play the beginning almost literally twice as fast as they did! We had a really tough time rehearsing and finding a way to combine these different approaches. But in the end, the process of trying to understand an opposing viewpoint and to find a viable compromise led to a performance that felt wonderfully alive because it contained so much tension and intensity. So that process of compromise can be not only a great learning process, it can also benefit the music. I find that very much with conductors, too—the etiquette is for the conductor to defer to whatever the soloist wants to do, but I quite like it when a conductor disagrees with me, and fights for his view of the piece. Then there's a different kind of engagement in the performance.

Do you get nervous when you perform?
Most of the time I don't get nervous at all, I just so enjoy making music, but when I do get nervous, it can be very intense. I feel that performance anxiety in musicians is an area that needs a great deal more attention. It's rarely, if ever, talked about in any meaningful sense at music colleges or among musicians themselves. Yet it seems that virtually all musicians suffer or have suffered with it at some point in their career. I find this a fascinating question—what is there to be nervous about? If you have prepared the music well, why should you doubt your ability to do on stage what you can do in the practice room? Musicians frequently crucify themselves for making minor errors that the vast majority of the audience probably didn't notice, and those that did almost certainly didn't care. I recently heard a beautiful performance of Mahler's Ninth Symphony, and when I went to see the musicians afterward they told me that the cellos and basses had got confused in the last movement and had played out of sync for about half a minute. I hadn't even noticed! If we musicians realized how little the audience judges us and how much they enjoy what we do, it would make our lives a lot easier. But perfectionism is rife among musicians, and it's difficult to uproot because it is so fundamentally connected to one's sense of self. I think that coming to understand these issues is enormously important for a performer because when one is very nervous, one is unable to connect properly with the emotions in the music.

Where do you enjoy playing?
The Wigmore Hall in London and the Queen's Hall in Edinburgh are two favorites. I grew up going to concerts at the Queen's Hall and played in many school concerts there. It has a lot of sentimental appeal for me but also is a

wonderful space: It has a good acoustic and is a good size for recitals. The Wigmore Hall is important to me for many reasons, not least that the first time I played in a real hall was there. I did a scholarship audition when I was 10, and the first note I played there is burned on my memory: I couldn't believe that a piano could sound so beautiful. The audience at the Wigmore is a very cultured one and very loyal, and the Hall management is a wonderful example of artistic integrity, not interested in glitz but caring primarily about musical values. I think that is part of the reason the Hall has such a devoted following among audience and musicians.

Thank you so much for sharing your time and thoughts in conversation today.
You're welcome.

Select Discography

Hyperion
Maurice Ravel. *The Complete Solo Piano Music.* Includes *La Valse.* Two discs. Notes by Osborne. Hyperion 67731/2. 2011.

Franz Schubert. *Duets.* With Paul Lewis. *Lebensstürme,* D. 947; *Andantino varié* in B Minor, D. 843 # 2; *Fugue* in E Minor, D. 952; *Rondo* in A Major, D. 951; *Variations on an Original Theme* in A-flat Major, D. 813; *Fantasie* in F Minor, D. 940. Hyperion CDA 67665. 2010.

Sergei Rachmaninov. *Morceaux de fantasie, op. 3; Preludes,* op. 23; *Preludes,* op. 32. Hyperion CDA 67700. 2009.

Benjamin Britten. *Piano Concerto* in D Major, op. 13; *Young Apollo:* Piano, String Quartet, and String Orchestra, op. 16; *Diversions* for piano left hand and orchestra, op. 21. BBC Scottish Symphony Orchestra. Ilan Volkov, conductor. Hyperion CDA 67625. 2008.

Charles-Valentin Alkan. *Cello Sonata* in E Minor. Frederic Chopin. *Cello Sonata* in G Minor. With Alban Gerhardt, cello. Hyperion CDA 67624. 2008.

Sir Michael Tippett. *Piano Concerto (1953–1955); Fantasia on a Theme of Handel; Piano Sonata # 1; Piano Sonata # 2; Piano Sonata # 3; Piano Sonata # 4.* BBC Scottish Symphony Orchestra. Martyn Brabbins, conductor on CD no. 1. Two discs. Hyperion CDA 67462. 2007.

Claude Debussy. *Preludes.* Books I and II. Hyperion CDA 67530. 2006.

Franz Liszt. *Harmonies poétiques et religieuses.* Two discs. Hyperion CDA67445. 2004.

Olivier Messiaen. *Visions de l'amen.* Osborne, Piano I, and Martin Roscoe, Piano II. *Solo: Pièce pour le tombeau de Paul Dukas; Rondeau; Fantasie burlesque.* Hyperion CDA 67366. 2004.

Olivier Messiaen. *Vingt regards sur l'enfant-Jésus.* Two discs. Hyperion CDA 67351/2. 2002.

Notes

1. Paul Lewis (b. 1972); Martin Roscoe (b. 1952); Alban Gerhardt (b. 1969); Nicola Benedetti (b. 1987); Dietrich Henschel (b. 1967).

2. Richard Beauchamp (b. 1946) began teaching at St. Mary's Music School in 1977. His website www.musicandhealth.co.uk is devoted to piano teaching and focuses on technique through the study of anatomy, biomechanics, and ergonomics. His name is pronounced "Beecham."

3. Renna Kellaway grew up in Durban, South Africa. At 17 she moved to Amsterdam, coming to England later.

4. Johannes Röntgen (1898–1969). Dutch pianist and composer known for playing with Pablo Casals. He taught at the Amsterdam Conservatory of Music from 1943 to 1953. Franz Osborn was a Berlin-born, Jewish pianist who later immigrated to England and died at age 49 in July of 1955 in London.

5. Robert Mann (b. 1920) was a founding member of the Juilliard String Quartet in 1946. He retired as its first violinist in 1997. He won a Naumburg award in 1941, later served as president of the Walter W. Naumburg Foundation, and has long served as a juror of the competition. Founded in 1925, the Naumburg Foundation is known for changing the rules for its competition winners as the cultural conditions for young artists have changed over the decades.

6. John Lill (b. 1944) came to international attention in 1970 when he shared the first prize in the Tchaikovsky Competition. This was at a time of a dearth of British pianists. He became known for playing, and his recording of, the complete cycle of Beethoven's sonatas.

7. Paul Crossley (b. 1944) was born in Yorkshire, England. As a pianist, he is known for playing the music of Messiaen, Nicolas Maw, George Benjamin, and most notably Tippett, who wrote his Third and Fourth Sonatas in close association with Crossley. In 2007 CDR Records released his two-disc recording of the sonatas.

8. Nicolai Petrov (1943–2011) on Olympia Recordings. A native Russian, at age 19 he took second prize at the Van Cliburn Competition in 1962. His goal was to introduce the music of neglected composers to audiences.

9. Julian Anderson (b. 1967) was born in London. His teachers include Goehr, Murail, Messiaen, and Ligeti. As a composer, he has held residencies with a number of major orchestras and was the Young Composer Fellow with the Cleveland Orchestra from 2005 to 2007, the same time he was professor of composition at Harvard. His music embraces traditional cultures far from that of Western music, with an inclination toward the folk music of Eastern Europe. He is most widely known for his symphonic compositions.

Yevgeny Sudbin. Photo by Greg Helgeson, courtesy of the Minnesota Orchestra

CHAPTER SEVEN

∼

Yevgeny Sudbin

Yevgeny Sudbin was born in St. Petersburg, Russia, on the 19th of April in 1980 to musical parents. At 30, his life falls easily into three distinct periods. His parents left Russia and sought asylum in Berlin for themselves and their two children in 1990, living in the basement of an old hospital for a time. Sudbin has remarked that at one point during this period he did not know whether he would ever play the piano again. But luck intervened when he received a piano as a gift, found a compatible teacher, and a Berlin mentor helped pave his way to London. There he graduated with his master's degree in 2005 from the Royal Academy of Music. He has been the recipient of numerous first prizes at international competitions and has received support from the Pulvermacher Foundation, the Wall Trust, and the Alexis Gregory Foundation as a Vendôme Prize winner.

Sitting close to the keyboard, his manner is undemonstrative and self-possessed, with little extraneous show during performance. Communicating with the audience through music is paramount. He made his London Wigmore Hall debut in February of 2005 and has since returned several times. His U.S. recital debut was at the Frick Collection in New York in December of 2006 as part of a tour of the United States and Canada.

Sudbin came to the attention of the wider music world after he recorded 18 sonatas of Scarlatti for the Bis label in Sweden's Västeras Concert Hall in October 2004. Sudbin spent a month, prior to recording, playing through all of Scarlatti's 500-plus sonatas deciding which ones to record. The recordings of both Vladimir Horowitz and Mikhail Pletnev[1] played a role in his leaning toward these elegant gems of this ingenious Baroque master. Worldwide acclaim led Bis to signing Sudbin to a five-year contract for further recordings.

I sat down for conversation with Sudbin in Minneapolis on the 4th of November in 2007 and on the 5th of October in 2008, both occasions after his concerto performances with the Minnesota Orchestra and Osmo Vänskä. He played Beethoven's Fifth Concerto first and returned the next fall for Beethoven's Fourth Concerto. After each performance he spoke enthusiastically about working with Vänskä and their continuing relationship, which brought them to record all five Beethoven concertos for Bis with the Minnesota Orchestra by 2012.

The music of Scriabin, Medtner, and Rachmaninoff holds a special interest for Sudbin. His relationship with Rob Suff at Bis led to his suggestion for a recording coupling the earlier version of Rachmaninoff's Fourth Concerto with Nicolai Medtner's Second Concerto. In September of 2008 Sudbin signed a new agreement with Bis to record 14 discs over a period of seven years. As part of this contract, he recorded the Rachmaninoff and Medtner concertos in Raleigh, North Carolina. He has also played Scriabin's concerto for a number of seasons, including with Neeme Järvi and the London Philharmonic Orchestra in 2009. As do a number of other pianists, Sudbin enjoys contributing his own liner notes to his recordings, which he has done with his Scarlatti and Scriabin recordings.

In our second meeting, Sudbin told me how he had recently come into possession of a cache of treasured items owned by Medtner who had lived in London since 1936 and died there. The items were almost destined for the landfill until a friend of the owner read about Sudbin's interest in Medtner and contacted him. Most valuable for Sudbin are the old 78 recordings, and original takes of Medtner playing his three concertos in the late 1940s, as well as his recordings of his songs with the soprano Elisabeth Schwarzkopf.[2]

In the fall of 2009 Sudbin took part in a documentary about the life of Medtner filmed for Russian television. The filming took place at the Royal Academy of London. The film gave Sudbin a chance to champion one of his favorite native composers by playing Medtner's music and featuring many of the treasures from his own Medtner collection.[3]

Although of a reserved and modest nature, Sudbin opened up further to speak excitedly about his BBC Proms debut in July of 2008 when he played Rachmaninoff's First Concerto with the BBC Philharmonic under Yan Pascal Tortelier. This performance captured the eye of the press. Much was made over the fact that early the morning after this Proms performance, he made a quick getaway to his wedding in Naples, and a honeymoon safari in South Africa. His wife, Sally Wei, is also a pianist and teacher; they have a young daughter, Isabella. He was appointed visiting professor of piano at the Royal Academy of Music in London in September of 2010.

Interview

Congratulations on your fine performance of Beethoven's Emperor Concerto last night with the Minnesota Orchestra! Is this your first performance with an American orchestra?

For me, this is my second appearance with an American orchestra. The first one was in the summer when I played the Beethoven concerto for the first time in Aspen with the Aspen Chamber Orchestra. So here in Minneapolis is the second. It's been fantastic. Actually, in my experience it's the best orchestra I've ever played with. Osmo Vänskä is wonderful. I can't believe it's over! It's been almost a week, but it's gone by so quickly.

How would you characterize the three performances that you've had here?

All three nights were different. The first night is always a bit more tense because you don't know what will happen. There can always be surprises in the first performance. The second night maybe had more energy, and the third performance was the most controlled.

You've arrived in Minneapolis with this performance of the Beethoven straight on the heels of playing it in Armenia. In Yerevan.

Oh, yes, that was quite the trip! I played there in the First International Festival in Armenia. It was like a warm-up for me. I'm glad I've done it, but the trip here was absolutely crazy. I've never had anything like that. Air France was striking in Paris. I was completely stranded in the airport and couldn't fly anywhere—for many hours. They wouldn't let us know what was happening. I went crazy just because I didn't know whether I'd make it. They sent the plane through Aberdeen, and I was fortunately able to make it here.

Were you not able to leave the airport?

No, no. I was glued to the board. The staff wouldn't tell us anything. They just said, "Look at the board." I did go to the train station to see whether I could catch a train to London, but they were all booked up. So I had to go back to the airport. It was a little bit like a black hole. I have to say, the traveling can be sometimes much more tiring and challenging than the playing because there are so many things you cannot control. Sometimes I arrive so exhausted that I just come out on the stage. And it does actually give me energy to be on the stage. I feel invigorated from the music just because the travel part can be so exhausting. But it's definitely worthwhile. It's more than that. It compensates me for these stresses I encounter when I travel. But I have to say the trip to Armenia was probably the worst I have encountered [*laughs*]. I can now laugh about it, but at the time it was terrible.

Let's talk about your youth. Your parents are both pianists.
Yes, my parents, Oleg and Lora Sudbin, met at the conservatory in St. Petersburg, as pianists. My mother later taught at a piano music school, but my father became ill during my youth. He passed away some years ago. Yes, as musicians, my parents encouraged me very strongly when I grew up. I had tremendous support from my mother. My first lessons were with my mother and continued with her until we started arguing, which was after maybe the third lesson [*laughs*]. After which, she took me to a specialist music school where I was accepted straightaway. From then things moved very quickly. A year or two later I won my first international competition, the Aussig Piano Competition. I was eight I think. So from then on, it became pretty serious. Because before, I don't think she even wanted me to play the piano. I started on my own initiative. I listened to the recordings of Richter and Gilels; we had lots of LPs. I improvised when I was four. Yes, at first it was more a leisure thing, but then quite quickly it became very serious.

Tell me about your move to Germany.
We moved to Germany when I was 10, and my mother and my sister live in Berlin now. My mother is now a private piano teacher. My sister also plays piano but is now a student studying sound engineering.

What pianists do you remember hearing during your youth in St. Petersburg?
Oh, yes, most vividly I remember hearing Evgeny Kissin,[4] who was my idol at that time. Whenever I went to concerts it was to hear him play, or whenever there was someone on the television playing it would be him. At that time it was really his golden years. It was really a privilege to hear him play at that time because I felt that he was a god.

Your first international competition was in Czechoslovakia. What did you play in that competition?
I remember that it was very stressful when I played. Yes, I think it was quite typical Russian repertoire. In Russia there is very serious training where every three months you change the repertoire you're playing. You play a Beethoven or Mozart sonata, a romantic piece, a contemporary piece. You always play a Bach prelude and fugue. There were some virtuoso pieces, for example, études. There was one technically difficult piece that I was struggling with for a long time.

After lessons with your mother, who was your teacher?

My mom took me to this Russian guru just to listen to me, to get her opinion. I remember that it was quite a big deal at the time because she was a big name in Russia at that time. Lyubov Pevsner. She took me to her apartment. I remember that her apartment was full of presents from all of her students who studied with her. The whole apartment contained presents that were everywhere! When I arrived in her flat I felt quite small. I played for her and at first she seemed quite cold, but later she warmed to me. She said I must come study at the special music school of the St. Petersburg Conservatory.

What music was she teaching?

Well, again, these varied programs from various periods. She hardly ever prescribed anything specifically for the technique, for which I was very grateful because I actually at the time struggled with my technique, which wasn't very good. By playing scales and by playing arpeggios, Czerny, for example, they would really show all the flaws in my playing. But she would give me difficult pieces. Chopin études, of course, came a little bit later, as I was only six or seven when I went to her. The main thing was that my technique improved greatly when I played pieces, not when I played mere études. When I didn't think about technique, but just thought about the music, I played better. The main objective was how to bring certain musical ideas across, and how you do that physically was, in a way, left up to me. When I didn't think about it in terms of technique but rather in terms of music, it actually happened much quicker. It was a shortcut for me, and worked very well. By thinking musically—how the phrases worked, where the climaxes are, in these sorts of musical terms—I improved.

What was the general musical life like in St. Petersburg in the mid-1980s? Was there a tight-knit community of young pianists?

Yes. I remember just going to the school and having lessons. I was pretty focused on the piano really because the specialist music school also has classes for general education. They had a "free schedule"—which means a student didn't have to go to certain classes if he had an important recital or concert coming up. You had to take exams for general education, but if I had a concert or a competition that was coming up then I had a good excuse not to be in the class.

Are you talking about theory classes?

No, this would have been math or physics as part of general education. The school was designed so that the primary focus was on the instrument that you played. I've never encountered anything like this anywhere else—where the student is to be completely focused on the thing that he does. If you're good at your instrument, then you are forgiven for not going to the other classes. They really make you focus. I was only there until I was 10. Then I went to Germany where I had actually developed problems because the school system in Germany is very strict. Yes, sometimes I began wondering if I was going to become a chemist or a physicist rather than a musician because academics are taken very, very seriously. And I did my A-levels in London. I have completed my general education. I think in Russia the standard for general education is very high, too. But again, they make you take all the exams. It's just that you have a choice about actually going to the classes. The teachers in Russia are very understanding if you don't go to their classes, whereas in other countries when the teacher notices that your focus is not on their class, they sometimes can get a bit spiteful and make it harder for you.

Why did your parents want to move to Berlin? I understand that you arrived there seeking asylum.
Yes, it's a complicated story. Partly there were political reasons. This was just before the fall of the Soviet Union in 1990, about the time the wall came down in Berlin. At that time a lot of Jewish families were leaving Russia. We were going to go to Israel originally but because my father had multiple sclerosis, the warm climate of Israel would have been very devastating for him. Because of my father's health we moved to Germany where he got very good treatment. Actually we left on a tourist visa because otherwise the Soviet Union wouldn't let us leave if they saw us taking too many suitcases. So we had to look like we were going on a short trip. So all we took was my music and very little else. We had to leave family behind, like my mother's parents, just to make it look like a temporary thing. I remember in the airport we were told not to look too sad, especially not to cry. Otherwise, they can just make you come back. Even after the Soviet Union fell, for a long time I couldn't go back because I would have had to go into the army. As long as I had my Russian passport, then I couldn't go back. Only when I got my German passport was it safer to go and that was after 14 years of being away that I did return to St. Petersburg.

Are your mother's parents still in St. Petersburg?
They came to Berlin a few years later. My grandmother has since passed away, but my grandfather is still living, now in the care of my mother.

What was the occasion for your first return to St. Petersburg?
I had a concert there in 2003. My mother came with me as well. It was pretty incredible. I was invited by my friend Alexis Gregory, the publisher of the

Vendôme Press, who ran the competition called the Vendôme Prize[5] where I won the second prize several years earlier. He invited me, after I kept saying it would be really wonderful to play in St. Petersburg again. He was holding his competition in St. Petersburg and said it would be a good opportunity for me to play. So he brought me over. I did a big recital there at the conservatory. The hall was completely full and people still remembered me. I played a lot of Scriabin, Scarlatti, Rachmaninoff, and Chopin. It was a great occasion. Everybody came backstage. They remembered me, but I didn't always remember their faces as I had been young when I left. I found it incredible that the atmosphere, the essence, was still there as I remembered it. In general, as far as St. Petersburg was concerned, the people were still the same, I felt, but the city had changed. It had become much more westernized. McDonald's was on every corner. They restored the essential part of St. Petersburg, but they hadn't done anything apart from the center, which is a shame. But the city is, in my opinion, still the most beautiful city in the world. The people are still very cultured. It was always a center of culture and it's still wonderful. I was very emotional when I returned, but at the same time I rather felt very happy.

In Berlin you studied with Galina Iwanzowa at the Hochschule für Music. What did she emphasize in her teaching?
With her, we actually worked quite a lot on technique. That was quite a difference from my teacher in St. Petersburg. This was actually a period where my technique improved a lot. But in a way I kept the same regimen—going through a lot of repertoire for the technique. Because the more music you play, the more you progress. Again, it was always a mixture of things. Chopin, along with Prokofiev, Rachmaninoff, Beethoven, Schumann, and Bach. Literally everything, including contemporary pieces. But I have to add that after a few years my teacher from St. Petersburg came over to Berlin as well. So I actually continued to study with her, which was a great help. It worked just fine working with two teachers.

You must have had a feeling of home to have her come to live in Berlin.
I enjoyed studying with her in Russia, and it was great to continue to study with her in Germany. I was very lucky. She still lives in Berlin. She's very old now. I continued with her until I left for London, and even then I come back from London to play for her.

When you were about 12 or 13—those years that become so very important in terms of practice—about how many hours were you devoting to serious work at the piano?

Well, as much as was necessary. I don't recall the exact number. But it was more like four or five hours, I think. More than six hours, I felt there was not much point because you're just working your fingers. Of course, when I went to school, in Germany, maybe four hours would be the maximum. I was in school from eight to three, so there's not much time to practice.

How old were you when you realized that this was going to be your life's work?
It hit me in different stages. First, on a different level, when I just started playing piano, at four or five. I really wanted to do it. Actually I didn't really know yet that it's going to become permanent in my life, but I certainly wanted to do it as a full-time thing. Then later on when I started entering competitions and playing concerts, when I was around 12 or 13—well, I wasn't sure whether it was something I was going to do for my whole life— but I couldn't imagine doing something else. I couldn't possibly imagine living without playing the piano. But then when I was 22 or 23, I started having some thoughts. I was just curious about what other people do with their lives because, in a way, I never had the choice. Well, I mean that I never had to choose. I see all the people in the university not knowing what they're going to do, and even then if they think they know what they're going to do, they always change it. They don't decide what job they're going to have until they're 30 or something. I always found that quite a curious thing because I felt I knew since I was born. I didn't know if it was a good thing or a bad thing. So I actually tried to understand and get a little bit into people's heads and understand how they think about their life and their life choices. And I started wondering what other things I could do in my life apart from playing piano, and see where my skills are. After a while, I stopped wondering, because when I played concerts, the music felt right. I decided it wasn't necessary to spend too much time trying to determine what else I'm good at.

It's one thing to play the piano well, and be able to teach, but it's another to be able to fulfill a career. Don't you feel that that takes another dimension to a personality?
Yes, but it is a balance. I cannot influence many things. The only thing I can influence is the level of my playing and that comes from hard work. I cannot influence the events that happen around it. So there is a lot of randomness going on. Well, there's a lot of luck involved. So if my career develops, and it is developing—it has always been developing—then I'm grateful for that. If it's not developing, then I would consider other options. But the point is I know there are things I have influence over and I know there are things that

I have absolutely no influence over whatsoever. Apparently it is about how my career progresses. I have no illusions about it. There are many talented people who don't have any career whatsoever.

What about your physical state, your mental and emotional state? Being able to deal with life.
Again, these are things I can actually influence. Like my physical well-being, I can more or less influence that. My mental state of mind, my training, my practicing are all things I can actually influence. But in terms of career, who hears you and what gives you further opportunities, who is in the concert, how they like it, and the necessary recommendations—all these things are outside of my control. Also this is all very subjective.

You're still a German citizen.
Yes. For me, it was important to have a European passport in order to travel.

You moved to London in 1997. London's quite a vibrant musical city.
Oh, yes. I think London is still the center of the music world.

Tell me about your study with Christopher Elton, first at the Purcell School and then later at the Royal Academy of Music. How did you make your way to study with him?
It was actually the recommendation from a friend, Christine Löwenstein in Berlin. She read a big article about me and my family after I won the Federal Music Competition ("Jugend Musiziert") soon after I arrived there. She became a friend of the family. She was quite determined and quite behind the idea that I should go to London. Actually, I don't think that just by myself I would have been able to go to London. She had heard many things about Christopher Elton. So I came over and had lessons with him and I liked him straightaway. I was really determined then to study with him.

While you were at the Royal Academy you worked with a number of visiting professors.
Yes, there, but I also went to Italy to Lake Como and attended the International Piano Foundation school. There were a great number of teachers there, including Leon Fleisher.

Tell me about meeting him for the first time.
He's incredible. I played Brahms for him. The wisdom you receive from a personality like his! It's just overwhelming. I remember that we worked on pulse

and the idea of how it determines everything. This was in the intermezzi, but I don't remember which one. It's just amazing how a tiny little division of pulse can destroy the whole musical structure. We worked a lot on that. I had a very different perception and he was very, very helpful. There were many teachers there I really enjoyed.

Tell me about working with Alexander Satz.[6]
Yes. I worked with him a lot on Scriabin. He came to the academy many times on a regular basis as a visiting professor. I think he was one of the greatest living teachers. He was a great influence on me especially with regard to Scriabin. Those were some of the best lessons I had. He had a tremendous brain, and it was a real shame that he has passed away. It was a tragedy.

I understand that his classes and lessons could be rather lengthy.
Oh, yes, they can go on for hours. Also he has this tremendous idea of color, and Scriabin is very important for color. I mean Satz just sits down and plays. If, for example, you're working on Scriabin, he can play all his works from memory. Satz has everything in his head. He isn't concerned with one piece, but with the whole composer. This means everything by the composer! He broadens your horizon. It was like I got new glasses! It's the same with Beethoven. He'd play all the sonatas and even the orchestra works.

Were those private lessons?
Sometimes private, and sometimes in a master class. I always prefer the private lessons, of course, because they are more intense.

How about Fou Ts'ong, who is originally from Shanghai?[7]
He was very, very nice.

Is he still teaching?
I think so. Rarely. He's still playing. That's for sure. I didn't have as many lessons with him. He came also to Italy and we worked on Chopin. He was very inspirational. We would sing a lot in lessons! And conduct. A lot of the music making was actually very physical. Every morning Fou Ts'ong did Tai Chi. Having classes with him was like having lessons in the martial arts!

Oh, yes! Music comes from the body.
Oh, it was great! The music making was very inspiring.

Stephen Hough has also been a visiting professor at the Royal Academy. When did you first meet him?

Actually, I met him through a competition when I was playing for the Vendôme Prize in London in 2000 and he was adjudicating. It was quite funny. He was on the jury, but I didn't know him then. The jury went out to deliberate, and he came out after about five seconds and announced that I had won. This was quite nice. After that, I spoke with him and we got along really well. Then he came to the academy, and I played for him in private lessons. He's actually quite the piano guru person. He knows all the tricks about the technical aspects of playing the piano, I found. Well, not just the technical aspects of course! I found it very interesting to hear from him about how he practices, how he sees certain passages, how to make it easier, how to think, how to bring out voices, and how to manipulate.

Do you remember how he practices?
Well, yes. For example, in Liszt, to get certain jumps right he would recommend practicing without the lights on. The idea behind this is that if you switch off one sense your other senses are more heightened. Also behind the idea of bringing out voices, you don't actually have to do it deliberately, but if you just think about the finger, it will happen automatically without your trying to do anything with force. You just think about the fourth finger, for example, and you can hear it. You don't have to especially press it harder or anything. A lot of it is very psychological. I also learned a lot about the practical things in how to prepare for concerts. You know, he is mainly a pianist, not a teacher. It's great to find out what he does.

He's such a master of tone color.
Yes. He really knows how to manipulate and negotiate the keyboard. He knows all the tricks and has helped me a lot.

He highly recommends that every pianist compose.
Well, I know he does, but I don't know that he recommends it.

As well, he makes transcriptions, and you yourself have made some transcriptions. Do you compose at all?
I used to compose when I was a child, but I no longer have time. It's a whole new profession and I want to focus on playing. But I do like writing some transcriptions for playing. And I have ideas, but I don't actually have the time to sit down and do it. But I will certainly find time in the future because it is something that I really enjoy.

Have you worked with Pletnev, or met him?
I met him, yes. But I never worked with him. I met him in Verbier at the festival in Switzerland. In Verbier he was mostly playing chess. There is a

big square in the middle of the town, and there is a big chessboard there. It's human size with big figures. He's there for hours playing chess.

I've been disappointed that he doesn't record more than he does, because he now devotes so much time to the Russian National Orchestra. So you've not played for him.
No. I'm not sure he does teaching. He's a great pianist.

He certainly is! You play Scarlatti, and Scriabin, and of course Rachmaninoff. And you're playing Haydn a lot. Are you going to record some Haydn?
Yes, definitely, I am. Hopefully, next year. I love him. For me, there is so much more imagination in Haydn's music than in the Mozart sonatas. Mozart's sonatas are about certain rules, but Haydn is all about breaking the rules. It is certainly outrageous music. Like Scarlatti.

Will there be more Medtner in the future?
Yes, I think he is a neglected composer. I would like to learn more of his music. The audience finds it sometimes hard, which is a shame. But if you know the music, it is just wonderful. It's just very hard to come to grips with it when you hear it for the first time. Unfortunately, you only get one chance to play it in the concert. When you really listen, Medtner is a wonderful composer. Pianistically as well as musically, there is a lot in Medtner, which is very rewarding for a pianist.

After listening to your recording of his C Minor Concerto, I admit that I find it difficult. It doesn't seem singable somehow.
It's a difficult piece. There are singable melodies but they are very complex. There are a lot of melodies that are not especially singable. You really wouldn't, for example, be able to sing the melodies of the second movement of the Emperor Concerto. In the Emperor you also have a melding of harmony and melody, and this is what actually makes it hard to sing. There isn't really a clear line of melody there. The underlying harmony is what gives life to the melody. You don't know where harmony ends and melody begins and vice versa. Also the colors in the Emperor's second movement are incredible because the harmony there is structurally the important thing.

Is there a living composer from whom you'd like to have a piece?
That's a good question. I'm always on the lookout for new music, but it's very hard to research because there are just so many contemporary composers. A lot of composers send me their music, and I always look at them. I did have

a nice encounter with Arvo Pärt, who is a wonderful composer. So perhaps if I had a piece from him.

What about the composers in Russia today, or in the former republics?
I know a lot of the composers, among them Shchredrin, of course. But I haven't played them. I am, however, always looking at new music.

What about live performance versus the recording studio?
I do like to record. I know a lot of performers don't find recording very stimulating, but there are different challenges when you are recording. I find that being in the recording studio I can reproduce the same state as being in a performance. You just have to reproduce it for eight hours in a row rather than a few hours. I do love recording because I think in performance you can hide a lot of things. I think that in a live performance things are more impressionable. I know it sounds strange, but people don't always get the impression about what I want to get across. Everything always moves quite quickly, and then people also often forget quickly. A recording is something you have permanently. Permanence in performance is something that I cherish because it doesn't really exist so much. I love recording. I think I can get my playing to another level, as well, in recording. In recordings one can't really hide anything. I know you can repeat things, but actually it is not a way to hide things. In a live performance there are too many tools. For example, people watch you, and sometimes don't even listen. They just watch you, and I find that quite disturbing. When I listen to concerts I usually close my eyes and listen to the sounds. I find the visual aspect can be a bit disturbing and sometimes confusing for the audience. If you listen to a recording of the same concert it can sometimes be completely different. And if you record, there is really nothing you can manipulate at all because it's right there. You can get rid of wrong notes, but you can't get rid of your musical understanding. If it's not of the highest order, then you can't probably hide it, no matter how many things you do.

You've worked with quite a few collaborators. For example, Julia Fischer, the young, highly regarded German violinist. How about singers?
I think the greatest is actually to play with a singer. I've only had once the experience of playing Mozart's great aria "Ch'io me scordi de te?" from *Idomeneo* with the Swedish soprano Miah Persson.[8] It's such an amazing piece when you have the two soloists and the orchestra there. It's actually such a romantic experience! Brendel and Schiff as well as others have played this aria. It is true that the biggest challenge for a pianist is to sing at the piano. I've never really sung, of course, but only on the piano! I do notice that when

I play the piano the natural intention is to sing, but I am a bit intimidated. There are, of course, some pianists who do sing sometimes at the piano, not just in their heads, and they're heard on recordings. I'd love to record Medtner's songs because he wrote some wonderful songs. He wrote more songs than Rachmaninoff did, and Rachmaninoff wrote about 100. Some of Medtner's best music is found in his songs. I'd love to do that!

Do you have an ideal singer in mind?
No. But, in the meantime, I'm challenging myself by transcribing songs for the piano. One is actually on one of my recordings. Again, this is my ambition of trying to make the piano sound like the voice. In thinking about songs and singing, I know that working with singers changes your piano playing quite a lot. With singers you are more aware of the singing qualities of the piano. Because while the piano is perceived as a percussion instrument, this is actually wrong. Certainly, it is technically percussive, but not a percussion instrument. Working with singers, you learn a lot about real singing qualities that you want to incorporate as a pianist, which is really enriching.

Are you a quick learner of music?
I think quite quick. It depends on how determined I am! I can learn pieces very quickly, usually in about a month. But I do take time, because even before I put my fingers on the keyboard I spend a lot of time thinking about the music before I actually learn it. Then the practicing comes but that doesn't take me long. It does take time for a piece to sink in. But for me, the best way to learn it is to learn it as fast as possible and perform it as many times as I can. Only through performance can you improve more, I find. If I put it aside without having performed it, it will go back. But if I learn it, and perform it, then it goes beyond a certain stage, and when I pick it up again it's much more fresh, I find. Performing is part of the learning experience. The more you perform a piece, the more you learn as well. I played the Emperor here three times and I felt that every performance was an improvement. Yes, the more I play a piece, the better it will be.

Let's talk about instruments. What instrument did you have in St. Petersburg?
I had an upright piano, a Red October,[9] which is a famous Russian brand. That's what I practiced on.

Then in Berlin you had a Steinway, perhaps?
I had a Steinway upright, which the conservatory actually gave me.

And today you have at home?
Oh, now I have a beautiful Hamburg Steinway B that I'm really happy with, and am really grateful that I have. It's fantastic to have a piano like that because it makes such a difference.

Do you know the Italian Fazioli?
Yes, but I do prefer Steinway. I find that the New York Steinway differs a lot from the Hamburg Steinway. The Hamburg Steinways are more consistent. Often I find it a bit tricky to play the New York Steinways because the range is slightly muffled and sometimes there is a lack of color. The two instruments differ quite a lot. A great New York Steinway can be incredible and much better than a Hamburg Steinway, but they are rare. The New York ones are generally more inconsistent and sometimes let me down in color because they need to cut through with an orchestra and still have the right colors. With the New York Steinway it can be very tough. The Hamburg instrument has more beautiful colors in the top region, and, in general, has more differentiation or a little more variety in color throughout the whole range. They are both wonderful instruments and for me are on a completely separate level, of course, from anything else.

Where do you find the best listeners in the world?
Maybe not where, but when. Those certain periods of the year when they don't cough so much!

What about the audience in a certain hall? For example, in Wigmore Hall.
Oh, yes, the audience in Wigmore Hall is very quiet and incredibly focused on what's going on. But it depends on various things, and varies from concert to concert. Sometimes you play in a huge hall and the audience is very noisy. It's quite distracting. But sometimes if you're playing for a less established music society, the people are very knowledgeable and pay attention much more. You never know.

Do you have some humorous stories about things that have happened while you're playing? Or has there been rude behavior that has forced you to stop?
No, that never happened. I always go on. But, yes, sometimes there is something very distracting going on. Somebody is either walking or talking. One of the last recitals I did was in a rather small hall when I played Medtner. On the stage, there was this outlet that exploded, and quite dramatically so. Quite loudly, like fireworks. There was a big black hole in the wall, which was pretty scary. I don't know how it happened.

Do you do yoga, or swim?

I do a bit of yoga, some back exercise, and some exercise in general. Swimming would be great, actually, but I'd have to find a place to swim. I don't swim. Exercise is very important, and nutritious food, too. I like to eat about four hours before a concert, but not too close. I eat carbohydrates and that sort of thing. After a concert I like to eat meat. Yes, I just make sure that I eat at regular intervals and not too heavily.

Do you still live in Middlesex, in London?

Yes, it's a county of London. It's actually still London, just on the outskirts, in the north. Where I live is very quiet and quite close to the city center. London is home for me, and even though I travel a lot, I do feel at home there.

Do you have time at all to take in drama and visit museums, or hear music, and other people play?

Yes, I do. I go to concerts. I don't like hearing another piano recital, so I try to go to something like chamber music concerts, or something completely different. If I play a lot, I don't want to hear so much piano music. If I have a holiday or something, then I might hear a piano recital. When I have time I go to the Alps to ski. I find that very invigorating, to get some fresh air and exercise at the same time. And you get the amazing view! Last year I went to France. Sometimes it's Switzerland or Austria.

Thank you so much for your time in sharing your insights with me.

Discography

Franz Joseph Haydn. *Sonatas*. # 47 in B Minor; # 60 in C Major; # 53 in E minor; *Fantasia* in C Major; Andante *con variazioni* in F Minor; Haydn, arranged by Sudbin: *Larking with Haydn*, a Pianistic Impression of the Finale of String Quartet in D Major. Liner notes by Sudbin. Bis-SACD 1788. 2010.

Sergei Rachmaninoff. Fourth Piano Concerto in G Minor, op. 40; Nicolai Medtner. Second Piano Concerto in C Minor, op. 50. North Carolina Symphony Orchestra. Grant Llewellyn, conductor. Liner notes by Sudbin. Bis-SACD 1728. 2009.

Alexander Scriabin. Étude, op. 8, # 12; Sonata # 2, (*Sonate-Fantaisie*), op. 19; Étude from *Three Pieces*, op. 2; Four Mazurkas, from op. 3; Sonata # 5, op. 53; Nuances from *Four Pieces*, op.56; Poème from *Two Pieces*, op. 59; Sonata # 9, *Messe Noire*, op. 68; *Valse*, op. 38. Liner notes by Sudbin. Bis-SACD-1568. 2007.

Mieczslaw Weinberg. Sonata # 1 for Cello and Piano, op. 21; Sonata for Solo Cello, op. 72; Sonata # 2 for Cello and Piano, op. 63. Alexander Chaushian, cello. Bis-CD-1649. 2007.

Peter I. Tchaikovsky. Concerto #1 in B Minor, op. 23; Medtner. Concerto # 1 in C Minor, op. 33; Medtner. "Liebliches Kind!" from his *Nine Goethe Songs*, op. 6, trans. by Sudbin. São Paulo Symphony Orchestra. John Neschling, conductor. Bis-SACD-1588. 2007.

Wolfgang A. Mozart. *Un moto di gioia: Opera and Concert Arias*. "*Ch'io mi scordi de te?*", K. 505. Miah Persson, soprano. Sudbin, piano. Swedish Chamber Orchestra. Sebastian Weigle, conductor. Bis-SACD-1429. 2006.

Domenico Scarlatti. *Eighteen Sonatas*. Liner notes by Sudbin. Bis-CD-1508. 2005.

Sergei Rachmaninoff. *Variations on a Theme of Chopin* (Prelude in C Minor, op. 28, # 20); Piano Sonata # 2. Transcriptions. Liner notes by Sudbin. Bis-SACD-1518. 2005.

Notes

1. Mikhail Pletnev (b. 1957). Born in Arkhangelsk in the Soviet Union. In addition to his two-CD recording of Scarlatti sonatas, he has made a specialty of Tchaikovsky's music. His transcriptions of excerpts from *Sleeping Beauty* and *Nutcracker* are virtuosic fantasies found on the Philips recording *Great Pianists of the 20th Century*. His enormous gifts as a conductor were behind his founding of the Russian National Orchestra at the time of the fall of the Soviet Union when he had backing from Mikhail Gorbachev and many in the United States.

2. The recordings were made under the sponsorship of Medtner's devoted sponsor, the Maharaja of Mysore, in London. Many of these recordings have been reissued.

3. Bhesania, Edward, "Great Expectations," *International Piano* (Mar./Apr. 2010), 18.

4. Evgeny Kissin (b. 1971). Born in Moscow. He is known for his virtuosity and his generosity to his audiences in giving numerous encores.

5. Alexis Gregory's foundation set up the Vendôme Prize International Piano Competition. The competitors are recommended from the leading international piano conservatories, and all participants are given ongoing career help.

6. Alexander Satz (1941–2007). Russian pianist and teacher who settled in Graz, Austria, in 1991. He taught at Graz's Academy of Music and Fine Arts. He had been a visiting professor at the Royal Academy of Music in London since 1999. Sudbin dedicated his Scriabin recording to his memory.

7. See Introduction for Fou Ts'ong.

8. Sudbin and Persson have recorded Mozart's concert aria on Bis. Mozart wrote the aria for the singer Nancy Storace's farewell concert in 1787 before she returned to England. Mozart was at the piano for this performance.

9. Red October is a Russian piano widely known in the Soviet Union era and in Russia today. Few made their way beyond the borders of the Soviet Union to Europe and other musical centers.

Yuja Wang. Photo by Xavier Antoinet

CHAPTER EIGHT

~

Yuja Wang

Yuja Wang was born in Beijing on the 10th of February in 1987 to artistically cultured parents. She well represents her generation of rising young Chinese artists who have flooded Western concert stages during the first decade of the 21st century. She follows in the footsteps of Lang Lang and Yundi Li, who were both born in 1982. The Dionysian Lang Lang, who preceded Wang by a few years at Curtis, made his initial impact in 1998, and has since morphed into a celebrity pianist; the Apollonian Yundi Li made his name playing Chopin after winning the Chopin Competition in 2000 and settled in Europe for years. He now resides in Hong Kong. Among their satellites are most notably Sa Chen (b. 1979), Mei-Ting Sun (1981), and Hao Chen Zhang (b. 1990), who was Wang's contemporary at Curtis. Zhang, who was born in Shanghai, also studied with Wang's teacher Gary Graffman[1] and became a co–gold medalist at the 2009 Van Cliburn Competition. Although each of these young Chinese pianists pursued advanced study either in the United States or Europe, many began their early piano studies with Chinese teachers who had studied a generation earlier in Europe and the Soviet Union. Wang's teacher Ling Yuan at Beijing's Central Conservatory of Music falls into this group. After her study in the West, Wang remains loyal to Yuan's teaching.[2]

After spending three summers, from 1999 to 2001, on a Canadian-Chinese artistic and cultural exchange program at the Morningside Music Summer Program at the Mount Royal College Conservatory in Calgary, Wang moved to Canada for study with Hung-Kuan Chen. She credits this period of isolation in her life to having found herself as a person through her time alone, learning English, reading and absorbing Western culture. During this time she developed her voracious appetite for exploration, a trait that has not left her.

Wang began her journey to international prominence in 2005 at age 16 while still a student at Curtis when she was called on a day's notice to substitute for Radu Lupu playing Beethoven's Fourth Concerto. After this successful performance, she received further last-minute calls for indisposed concerto soloists, such as Martha Argerich and Murray Perahia. In the spring of 2008 Wang joined the Academy of St. Martin's in the Fields on their U.S. tour, substituting for Perahia. For this tour she performed Mozart's C Minor Concerto, K. 491, playing her own cadenzas. She later remarked on a number of occasions that substituting was becoming her profession. Her willingness and ability to fill in at the last moment led to signing her own professional management in 2005. Shortly thereafter, she signed a contract for five recordings with Deutsche Grammophon. In a few short years she had played with many of the world's best orchestras, including the Boston Symphony Orchestra, the Chicago Symphony Orchestra, the New York Philharmonic, and San Francisco Symphony in the United States, and internationally with the Tonhalle Orchestra, the China Philharmonic, and the NHK Symphony in Tokyo. As well, she has made numerous appearances at leading international festivals, most notably the Santa Fe Chamber Music Festival, the Verbier Festival, the Gilmore Festival, and the Lucerne Festival. In 2006 Wang received the Gilmore Young Artist Award, and in 2010 she was awarded an Avery Fisher Career Grant for exhibiting "great potential for a solo career." Without competing or winning a major international piano competition, and apparently without serious consideration of developing a career, she has risen to international prominence. In the midst of her active performing schedule, she continued her studies at Curtis and graduated in 2008.

Early in 2009, the London Symphony Orchestra, with other notable music institutions, held worldwide auditions for amateur musicians to participate in a performance of the YouTube Symphony Orchestra. Wang joined violinists Joshua Bell and Gil Shaham, as well as composers Mason Bates and Tan Dun at the YouTube Symphony Orchestra's performance under Michael Tilson Thomas at Carnegie Hall in April of 2009. Wang played the scherzo movement from Prokofiev's Second Concerto, and as an encore she offered Cziffra's[3] transcription of Rimsky-Korsakov's "Flight of the Bumblebee." Her playing of this transcription and Volodos's[4] *Turkish March*, his transcription of Mozart's *Rondo alla turca* from the A Major

Sonata, K. 331, became two of Wang's most viewed videos on YouTube by the end of the first decade.

I spoke with Wang about the concert in which she fell under Mahler's spell when she heard his First Symphony played by the Lucerne Festival Orchestra with Claudio Abbado. Wang was in Lucerne as soloist with the orchestra to open the August 2009 Lucerne Festival playing Prokofiev's Third Concerto in C Major. After these performances Abbado took the orchestra and Wang to Beijing for five days in September of 2009. Their performances took place at the National Center for the Performing Arts, which opened in 2007 and had quickly become one of the most visible indications of China's rise in the musical world.

Despite her petite build, Wang exhibits tremendous physical stamina at the piano. Her artistry comes with great flair, panache, and a streak of near fearlessness. Indeed there is an edgy abandon in her playing.

I spoke with Wang by phone on the 15th of February 2010 after she had flown to Portland, Maine, where she was to appear the next evening with the Portland Orchestra playing Rachmaninoff's Second Piano Concerto. She had just completed two performances with the Shanghai String Quartet in one weekend in Detroit and Richmond, Virginia. With her tight schedule, it had not been easy to arrange a time to speak together. I discovered a bright, optimistic, natural young artist completely at ease with herself. Great confidence lends her an easy, frequent laugh with a bit of mischief in her tone. As a 21st-century communicator, she actively uses Twitter. While she takes making music very seriously, she doesn't take herself seriously. She is philosophical enough to realize she will not always be a young pianist but must continue to mature as an artist.

Interview

Where do you call home today?
I live in New York City today. I left home when I was 14 and my parents did not come with me. They are still living in Beijing, and I visit them only when I have concerts in China. They have jobs and don't have time to travel often, but they did hear me once in Philadelphia when I was graduating from Curtis. But I am in close touch with them and call them all the time.

Your father, Jianguo Wang, is a percussionist in an orchestra, and your mother, Zhai Jieming, was a ballet dancer with the China National Ballet. Does she still dance today?
No, she does choreographic and design work now. And she does yoga.

Did you grow up learning yoga?
I actually started as a dancer, but she said I wasn't flexible enough, because, you know, a dancer's life is really hard. So I took up piano instead.

How did you discover the piano as a child?
My mom plays a little piano. The instrument at home was actually a gift to her from my dad. So I started learning it as a hobby, like calligraphy, study in art class, and dancing. My mom was my first teacher. She taught me how to read music. It was great because she's a dancer and she knows how the physical aspects work—things like how to relax and not be tense. I was probably with her about a half year, or perhaps a little longer, and then she found a teacher for me when I was seven.

What kind of instrument did you have growing up in China?
I was lucky. I had a Yamaha that was rebuilt by Steinway, so it was really a Steinway. It was a red piano and I really liked it. Later in Calgary I had a Kawai. And now after Curtis, I have a great New York 2002 Steinway model B. I used to have a 1920 Hamburg Steinway, but it was way too old and I gave it up because it needed to be rebuilt. But in China, most people have one of those Chinese pianos, and they're just a block of wood.

Have you had much experience with the Fazioli piano?
I did try one in Calgary where they have a shop. It was nice, but I felt that it was too glassy and clear for some repertoire, and most of the time I felt like I was walking on eggshells. The action is light.

Returning to your youth in Beijing, did you have a chance to hear pianists in recital live or with orchestras?
I went to a lot of ballet rehearsals and heard music. My first teacher was actually the accompanist with the China National Ballet where my mom was working. I went to lots of those rehearsals. I was actually more interested in the symphonic side of music, and I started learning about the clarinet, the oboe, and all the other instruments. They interested me. My dad was in a different orchestra, not this one with the ballet. I was surrounded by music from the beginning of my life.

Were you listening to recordings at home during this time?
No, not until I went to the conservatory in Beijing when I was 10. They had amazing CDs there. I didn't even own any CDs until I was 10. The first thing I listened to was Rubinstein's recording of Chopin nocturnes, and I remember

how shocked I was. I said, "Oh, this is how other people play the piano." The second CD I had was Pollini's Chopin études, and I became a big fan of his.

At the conservatory you studied with Ling Yuan. Tell me about her.
I was with her at age 10 until I left China when I was 14. She was Russian trained. Her husband, Zhao Guanren, was Lang Lang's teacher. So when she was on a trip or on vacation I had lessons with him. He was Russian trained, too. My teacher was really interested in German music; Beethoven and Chopin were her favorite composers and later Brahms. So I guess perhaps she's more European, than Russian, actually. I'm not sure whether she studied in Russia, but I know her husband studied with a student or a relative of Scriabin. He really knows this area of music.

What was Ling Yuan's teaching like?
She was very sensitive and had great taste in music. She showed me all her recordings, which represented just the top artists. She would never let me listen to bad artists. She was really into sound as well, which is the Russian aspect. She stressed how to listen, how to produce a sound, and to pedal, and generally just how to be a really good musician, instead of just how to play fast. For some reason when I was younger, my first teacher, the accompanist at the ballet classes, said "I don't think she can play the piano. Her fingers are too skinny." So Ling Yuan started training my strength. Part of her teaching included some of the same things my mom had taught me about the body. She didn't concentrate on just a few things, but she put it all together very well. Everything goes with the music. She chose lots of good repertoire for me. I had an amazing time learning so much repertoire with her. She always let me play things until they really sank in and were really digested. Which is unlike my training here in America. Here I just played different pieces all the time, which is good, too, because my repertoire really grew. I think that I can always come back a few years later to let it sink in.

While you were at the conservatory you made several trips to play in Germany, Spain, and Australia. How were these trips arranged and did you go by yourself?
I played as part of competitions on those trips. Every country is different, but my trips were part of Chinese cultural exchanges and I was part of larger groups of students who were also on these trips at this time. Of course, I had to audition in China for the chance to go. My parents didn't come with me, but the Chinese government had chaperones who came with the students on these trips.

Were you studying English at this time?
We had English in school, but not very much. The alphabet! I knew how to say "How are you?" The year when I was in Calgary at age 14 and 15 is when I really starting speaking.

When you were about 12, 13, and 14, about how many hours a day were you devoting to practice?
Oh, two, three, or four hours—depending.

Nothing outrageous like five or six?
[*laughs*]

Was it difficult for you to practice on a daily basis, or were you eager to do it?
When I was younger, my mom always told me that it was through practice that all the instruments are learned and that I really had to do that. It didn't take me too much to do as she asked. I liked it.

I know that you yourself are so interested in music as a broad field and that piano is just one single part of music for you personally. For some young children, focusing solely on the piano can be tedious. Frequently, young children don't understand the value of spending a lot of time at things that seem boring and uninteresting to them, and only when they get a little older, perhaps in their teens, do they begin to realize the value of serious work at the piano.
Actually for me it was backward. It's harder for me now than when I was younger because now there are so many more fun things to do. When I was young it was more interesting to practice than to do homework. I would rather practice!

Can you remember a point when you realized that you were going to be a professional pianist rather than this being a hobby?
It's weird because I never really thought about it. I just kept playing and realized that it was just a natural thing for me to play on the stage. It developed easily out of my playing when I was very young. So, yes, while it is naturally a part of me, I am actually now trying to make it less so for the world in order that I can make it exciting and fresh.

And if you were not a pianist, what do you think you might be pursuing?
I was very good at math when I was in school, but there are so many other things I could be doing. I like art, so I could be painting, or do fashion design,

which I'm thinking I should do [*laughs*]. I had thought about being a model, but I am way too short for that [*laughs*]!

Let's return to your early experiences in Calgary. You spent some time there before you moved there, didn't you?
Yes, during the summers. After moving there, of course, it was different in the winter. It was freezing!

Can you remember your thoughts about adjusting to this different life and culture?
First of all, it wasn't hard to leave my parents! Everyone was ready to leave his parents. At that age you just can't wait! Learning English was a big part of life, and it was so quiet there. There was a lot of time to focus on my inner self, to learn how to develop, and I started to be very independent. I was really curious about everything. I used the library a lot to check out books. Learning English evoked all my other interests, which was really nice. When I went to Aspen that summer for nine weeks that really helped my English. During that time there was a lot of self-doubt, too, on my part. I would think: "Am I playing this right?" or "If my teacher in China heard me play like this, is that good?" I still have those doubts a lot. In Calgary, my teacher Hung-Kuan Chen[5] was really different since he himself is an accomplished concert pianist. He doesn't teach at all like my teacher who was really devoted and made sure I had lesson time. I was personally in love with her. I pretty much had only five lessons with Chen during the whole year. I felt like I was left on my own, which sometimes is not a bad thing because I tried really hard to see what I could do on my own by experimenting. It was interesting for me because the teaching styles of various different teachers are so different. At Curtis, too. But now I'm used to that, and if people tell me what to do now I get rather offended because I know what to do.

With Chen how did that go?
I rather knew what I wanted to do. But then again, I realized that I could learn so much from him. He had so much experience since he had gone to Germany to study when he was 13. His repertoire list was the compass of Beethoven, for example. So he really knows these pieces and knows how to play them, which was different for me because he could demonstrate very well. I worked on Beethoven with him. I remember a special lesson with him just before I auditioned for Curtis. I had the feeling that he is a mystic. Rather mysterious. What's the word? He always talked about energy, and he has this amazing concentration when talking about music. He was really

great at talking about music, too. Time didn't matter to him and sometimes these lessons went on forever. Also, I didn't work on any technical aspects of playing at all. In fact, he was amazed and would say, "How do you play that fast?" I already knew how to do that from my early training. My teacher in China was more intuitive, very imaginative, poetic, and knew how to relate everything together, too. Chen was teaching just a very few students in Calgary, I think. His wife, Tema Blackstone, is also a pianist. I seem to have lots of those! She was actually one of his students, but older than he is. She was like a mother figure for me that year. She helped out when he was not there, but not in an artistic way.

Chen suffered an injury after a ladder fell on his right hand, and he was forced to give up playing for several years. It's been reported that he developed focal dystonia after this accident.
That nobody can tell. I know he could practice 14 hours a day. It was amazing because it was probably not hurting him. Yes, there was a time when he couldn't play, and this is why he always talked about energy. He felt like Qi Jong helped him to heal the pain and return to playing. Another thing is that he really hates publicity. I think he tried to confuse people who would ask about his injury. He's a very inward person, and he likes to keep it that way. He was teaching in Shanghai last year, but he's now teaching again in Boston.

Were you able to make serious friendships with the other students you were in close contact with during those years?
Only at Curtis. I didn't have much in the way of friendships in China. Curtis was amazing, as every one there is a little genius! We played music all the time. I was friends with players who played many different instruments. But at Curtis it was different because I played frequently with others. I love cello, for example, and clarinet. In fact, I love playing in a group. Later at Curtis, I worked with a group that included a clarinetist, and I played Bartók's Sonata for Two Pianos and Percussion. There is so much energy at Curtis. At Calgary I didn't have much contact with colleagues. And in fact I enjoyed being on my own during that time at Calgary. I have a guardian, Paul Dornian, who is a clarinetist who teaches at the conservatory. He's actually the director of the conservatory. He's not a pianist but he knows piano repertory, and he has a good outlook on life. He doesn't like to admit that! But, you know, it was nice to be without musicians for a year. My guardian is probably the most knowledgeable person I know and all his friends are, too. They know about everything! His wife, Kathy, is also amazing.

After you played at Aspen and auditioned, you were accepted at Curtis to work with Gary Graffman. Can you remember the first time you met him?
Yes. It was in my audition. I had seen lots of photos of him and I thought he was this humongous guy. But then he showed up and he was only just a little taller than me! I remember that at the audition I was all nervous. Then he called and said, "You're accepted at Curtis, and you're going to study with ME." I then felt really accepted. First of all I didn't know whether I would go to Curtis, and I certainly didn't know that HE would accept me.

Tell me about your lessons with him.
I always just played through my pieces for him. I had to have my own interpretation and have them ready at concert level, though not necessarily memorized at each lesson. After that, I felt, "Oh, okay. This is how it is. I have to work harder." I got used to it after a while. Thinking about differences here, for example, when I was in China I didn't have to be ready with a piece because the teacher would help me to get ready.

Did Graffman advocate yoga, Alexander Technique, or swimming as part of his overall teaching? I bring this up because he, too, like your teacher Chen, injured a hand. Did his teaching stress the promotion of things that will help toward avoiding injuries and stress on the body?
No. Injuries just happen. Some people have higher endurance and some people don't. And he really had been practicing so hard. You know, Leon Fleisher had the same problem. Too many concerts with big orchestras and they're really intense, so they practice like crazy. And because on most pianos the upper registers don't sound as big as the bass part of the piano, they injure their right hands.

When you arrived at Curtis in 2002 Lang Lang, who also studied with Graffman, had already left. Was his shadow still in the hallway?
Hmm, sort of.

Graffman has commented on occasion that your generation of pianists, and especially those from Asia and China, learn music so much more quickly than the pianists of his generation when they were your age. Do you have any thoughts on why this may be?
I'm not sure. But probably because we're being trained well, and we started early. And we listen to recordings so much. Most of us learn pieces really quickly. It's just the way we've been brought up and trained in Asia.

Do you think that perhaps Asian students have the ability to focus and concentrate for longer periods than perhaps others?
Yes, probably.

They have a longer attention span?
Which I don't have [*laughs*]! But, yes, Graffman always talked about how quickly Lang Lang and I learned pieces. He always said, "Everyone else is fast, but you guys are really fast."

While in Philadelphia, who did you hear playing that you really admire?
Actually, I really like Horszowski[6] a lot; I have recordings of his. I went every week if I could to hear the Philadelphia Orchestra; Curtis offered that. There were always great recitals with pianists like Emanual Ax and Yefim Bronfman. Valery Gergiev toured with an amazing orchestra, and I tried to get to as many concerts as possible. And even now, I try to hear as much as possible while living in New York as well. You know, Curtis has the best library, and there I came to admire Cortot.

You played the premiere of Jennifer Higdon's[7] piano concerto. Did you work with her at all during the time she wrote the piece?
No, not at all. She actually wrote it for Lang Lang. For some reason it didn't work out, so I had to premiere it. It was pretty much there. I got the music and she said, "If there is anything you need to change because it's unpianistic, tell me."

And were there unpianistic spots?
It was unpianistic the whole way. Now she's thinking about recording it, with me as the soloist, but the details are undecided at the moment. It's a great piece. Jennifer's piece was the second time I've premiered a piece—last December. This was at the Kennedy Center with the National Symphony Orchestra and Andrew Litton. Last summer at the Verbier Festival in Switzerland I premiered Rodion Shchedrin's[8] solo pieces, *Artless Pages*. They are seven little pieces reminiscent of Schumann's *Kinderszenen*. My experience was totally different with Shchedrin as I got with him every day until the premiere. He really knew the way he wanted it, but with Jennifer it was just "Do whatever you want. I'll enjoy my piece. I don't know how it's going to sound." I enjoyed both pieces, but they were very different. Neither was very complicated, or avant-garde, like the music of Ives or Ligeti.

Is there a composer you admire today from whom you'd love to have a piece written for you?
I've asked Mason Bates[9] to write a 15-minute solo piece for me. I met him through the YouTube Symphony. He was a DJ, and he is amazing. He combines electronics with weird classical music. It's really useful-sounding music, not particularly mature or profound but rather fun, other-worldly, and funky. Even a little rock 'n' roll.

Is there underrated earlier music that the public doesn't hear often enough, but that you feel should?
Oh, I'm sure there is a lot. I've played a little Medtner and definitely Scriabin, but they're not underrated at all. I love Scriabin, Stravinsky, and Prokofiev.

Your first recording, _Sonatas and Études,_ has become well known and received attention by its Grammy nomination several weeks ago. And you've recently returned from Hamburg where you recorded your second CD, _Transformation,_ which will be released this spring.
Yes. This recording contains Brahms's _Paganini Variations,_ Stravinsky's _Petrushka,_ Ravel's _La Valse,_ and several Scarlatti sonatas.

On your first recording you play two of Ligeti's now-famous études. I know you admire Ligeti's music very much. Is there a chance you may record all of his études one day?
Oh, that is a big undertaking [_laughs_]! I've not thought about it at all.

Yes, it is. Ligeti stretches one's brain! The first time I heard Aimard's recording I was incredulous, thinking, "This can't be!"
Now I just give up on them because I think electronics can do the music so much better than I!

In addition to the two brilliant transcriptions you frequently play as encores, you play a slow, heartfelt melodic transcription that you yourself made.
Yes, I do like transcriptions. This one I based on an aria in Gluck's opera _Orpheus and Eurydice._ It's called "Melodie," and depicts the scene right after Orpheus turns around and discovers that his Eurydice has disappeared.

Let's talk about an artist's individuality. What do you bring to keeping piano music alive and healthy today that is really distinctive on your part? What sets you apart from other pianists playing today?

Oh, I don't know! There is a big Asian boom right now, and people always expect us to be very clean and solid. I think the sensitivity on my part that I developed early with my first teacher really goes a long way. This came from her because she was more oriented toward European technique. In concerts I always want to have more electricity and this energy thing going on. That's what an audience expects, I think.

I know you're interested in many aspects of music, not just piano music.
Yes, I love symphonic music, especially Mahler's symphonies. I'm so lucky! The first time I heard Mahler's First was last year at the Lucerne Festival with the Lucerne Festival Orchestra, under Claudio Abbado, and then I heard Mahler's Second Symphony with the Concertgebouw at the Salle Pleyel in Paris, with Mariss Jansons, and so I fell in love with Mahler. Those two concerts were memorable. Right now I'm regretting that Mahler didn't write anything for the piano. I can memorize the Beethoven *Eroica* Symphony, of course. Liszt did transcriptions of Beethoven's symphonies, but they are much better with the orchestra than on the piano.

Recently, after your Grammy nomination, you spoke with Audi Cornish of NPR.[10] During the course of your conversation with her you made the comment that you didn't like to play the piano. You said, "I love music. I don't like to play the piano. It's just an instrument. Music intrigues me. I love opera, ballet, and symphonic music." I wonder whether you would expand on your comments for many who may have heard these words coming from you but had trouble understanding exactly what you are saying.
Yes, that was a rather stupid remark to make on NPR. What I meant was it's not piano that I want, but it's the music that I want. I don't want to play the piano, I want to play music, which is first. As well, it's about musicianship, not about technique, which is merely a means toward the music.

Well put. What do you see ahead for your country in the next 10 or 20 years as far as cultural life? Do you see a lot of Chinese pianists who are being educated in the United States and in Europe perhaps returning to China?
Yes. It's amazing because all those people come here and get the best education. There really is no difference if you get it in China or in America, but perhaps you get more discipline in China. It's really scary what all these students are going to be. There are so many, and they're really competitive.

Do you see yourself returning one day to China?
I haven't thought about it.

Have you encountered times when you must address an audience's behavior?
I just don't care anymore [*laughs*]. It always depends on what you expect. In China there is a lot of talking, but I don't play there very often. I don't even mind it if people clap between every single movement because a lot of people don't come to concerts and if they come and want to express themselves, it's okay. As long as they appreciate what I do, I don't care about those things.

Discography

Sergei Rachmaninov. *Rhapsody on a Theme of Paganini*, op. 43. *Piano Concerto # 2 in C Minor*, op. 18. Mahler Chamber Orchestra. Claudio Abbado, conductor. Deutsche Grammophon B004KD5TPY. 2011.

Transformation. Igor Stravinsky. Three movements from *Petrouchka*; Scarlatti. Sonata in E Major, K. 380, Sonata in F Minor/C Major, K. 466; Brahms. *Variations on a Theme by Paganini*, op. 35, Books I and II; Ravel, *La Valse*. Liner notes by Michael Church. Deutsche Grammophon B0014108-02. 2010.

Sonatas and Études. Frederic Chopin. Piano Sonata # 2 in B-flat Minor; György Ligeti. Étude # 4; *Fanfares*, Étude #10: *The Sorcerer's Apprentice*. Alexander Scriabin. Piano Sonata #2 in G-sharp Minor. Franz Liszt. Piano Sonata in B Minor. Deutsche Grammophon B0012534-02. 2009.

DVD

Sergei Prokofiev. Piano Concerto #3. Gustav Mahler. Symphony #1. Lucerne Festival Orchestra. Claudio Abbado, conductor. Recorded live in August 2009. EuroArts DVD 2057968. 2010.

Notes

1. See Introduction for Gary Graffman.
2. See Introduction for discussion of China and Chinese pianists.
3. György Cziffra (1921–1994). Hungarian pianist endowed with great bravura abilities.
4. Arcadi Volodos (b. 1972). Soviet-born pianist known for his thundering technique. Wang's YouTube clip of his *Turkish March* has remained popular.
5. Hung-Kuan Chen (b. 1958 in Taiwan) studied with Hans Leygraf and Alfons Kontarsky in Cologne, and later with Bela Boszormenyi-Nagy in Boston. He gave a

series of recitals of all 32 Beethoven sonatas in Boston in 1989. He later taught at the Shanghai Conservatory, but soon returned to teaching in Boston.

6. Mieczyslaw Horszowski (1892–1993) was born in Poland and came to the United States where he taught at Curtis. He had an extremely long career.

7. Jennifer Higdon (b. 1962) was born in Brooklyn. She teaches composition at Curtis and is an active composer whose music, especially her orchestral works such as *Blue Cathedral*, is widely performed. She won the Pulitzer Prize for music in 2010 for her *Violin Concerto*.

8. Rodion Shchedrin (b. 1932) was born in Moscow and became a well-accepted Soviet composer. Today he lives in Munich and is widely known for his operas, orchestral works, and six piano concertos. He is a pianist.

9. Mason Bates, born in Virginia, is today a thirtysomething composer who lives in San Francisco and is known there as DJ Masonic. Juilliard trained, he has married traditional orchestral music to electronic, having composed for the Pittsburgh Symphony Orchestra and the Los Angeles Philharmonic, among others. Hao Chen Zhang recorded his *White Lies for Lomax* for solo piano.

10. NPR broadcast on Saturday, 23 Jan. 2010.

~

Bibliography

Ashley, Douglas. *Music Beyond Sound: Maria Curcio: A Teacher of Great Pianists*. American University Studies Series XX. Vol. 19. New York: Peter Lang, 1993.

Bloom, Benjamin S., ed. *Developing Talent in Young People*. New York: Ballantine Books, 1985. See here, especially, Lauren A. Sosniak. *Leaning to Be a Concert Pianist*.

Crombie, David. *Piano: A Photographic History of the World's Most Celebrated Instrument*. San Francisco: Miller Freeman Books, 1995.

Dubal, David. *The Art of the Piano: Its Performers, Literature, and Recordings*. 3rd ed., rev. and exp. Pompton Plains, NJ: Amadeus Press, 2004.

———. *Reflections from the Keyboard: The World of the Concert Pianist*. 2nd ed. New York: Schirmer Trade Books, 1997.

Ericsson, K. Anders, Neil Charness, Paul J. Feltovich, and Robert R. Hoffman, eds. *The Cambridge Handbook of Expertise and Expert Performance*. New York: Cambridge University Press, 2006.

Fleisher, Leon and Anne Midgette. *My Nine Lives: A Memoir of Many Careers in Music*. New York: Doubleday, 2010.

Great Pianists in Conversation with Carola Grindea. London: Kahn & Averill, 2007.

Kraus, Richard Curt. *Pianos and Politics in China: Middle-Class Ambitions and the Struggle over Western Music*. London: Oxford University Press, 1989.

Mach, Elyse. *Great Contemporary Pianists Speak for Themselves*. New York: Dover Publications, 1990. This was originally published in two volumes, the first in 1980 and the second in 1988. The very young Stephen Hough was interviewed by Elyse.

Marcus, Adele. *Great Pianists Speak*. Neptune City, NJ: Paganiniana Publications, 1979.

Noyle, Linda J., ed. *Pianists on Playing: Interviews with Twelve Concert Pianists*. Metuchen, NJ: Scarecrow Press, 1987.

Pellegrini, Nancy. "The Man Who Saved the Piano for His Country." *International Piano* 1 (May/June 2010): 14–15.

Rimm, Robert. *The Composer Pianists: Hamelin and the Eight*. Portland, OR: Amadeus Press, 2002.

Yoshihara, Mari. *Musicians from a Different Shore: Asians and Asian Americans in Classical Music*. Philadelphia: Temple University Press, 2007.

Index

~

About the Author

Caroline Benser lives in La Crosse, Wisconsin, where she teaches piano and writes as an independent music historian. Her interest in contemporary European and American history, with a special focus on biography and oral history, served as the basis for her biography of Austro-English composer and musicologist Egon Wellesz and later her bio-bibliography, with David Francis Urrows, of American composer Randall Thompson. From 2006 to 2010 she served as the recording-review editor of the journal *American Music*.